WEST POINT
LEADERSHIP
LESSONS

DUTY,
HONOR,
AND OTHER
MANAGEMENT
PRINCIPLES

WEST POINT LEADERSHIP LESSONS

DUTY,
HONOR,
AND OTHER
MANAGEMENT
PRINCIPLES

SCOTT SNAIR

SOURCEBOOKS, INC.®
NAPERVILLE, ILLINOIS

Published by Sourcebooks, Inc.
P.O. Box 4410, Naperville, Illinois 60567-4410
(630) 961-3900
FAX: (630) 961-2168
www.sourcebooks.com

Library of Congress Cataloging-in-Publication Data

Snair, Scott.
  West Point leadership lessons : duty, honor, and other management principles / by Scott Snair.
      p. cm.
  Includes bibliographical references and index.
  ISBN 1-4022-0265-2
  1. Leadership. 2. Management. 3. Communication in management. I. Title.
HD57.7.S686 2004
658.4'092—dc22

Printed and bound in the United States of America
LB 10 9 8 7 6 5 4 3 2 1

FOR MARY-JANE

CONTENTS

FOREWORD

Several years ago, an article appeared in the *Wall Street Journal* that said the United States military academies were the best business schools in the nation. West Point? A business school?

The mission of the United States Military Academy is:

To educate, train, and inspire the Corps of Cadets so that each graduate is a commissioned leader of character committed to the values of duty, honor, country; professional growth throughout a career as an officer in the United States Army; and a lifetime of selfless service to the nation.

Again—a business school? On the other hand, perhaps the connection between good military management and good management in general is distinct and worth exploring. Scott Snair captures that essence as he looks at the common leadership characteristics among Academy alumni of yesterday and today. Are the characteristics revealed by great managers the same as those exhibited by successful leaders in combat? Can one draw an analogy between victory in war and victory in business? Just what are some of those common management characteristics? Certainly not an exhaustive list, the following descriptors capture the core of what one expects from a West Point graduate:

- Displays absolute integrity
- Maintains technical competence
- Takes care of subordinates
- Respects others

- Is goal-oriented
- Sets high standards for self
- Possesses supreme confidence
- Shows superb "people skills"
- Chooses leadership over "managership"
- Has high physical and mental drive
- Holds the ability to choose the "harder right" over the "easier wrong"

Given the moral degeneration that our nation has recently experienced in some high-profile corporations, it is no wonder that the West Point graduate has become a hot commodity in the "headhunting" business. Employers value the skills brought to the table by the alumni from West Point. Perhaps that is why Scott Snair's book is a must-read for any manager trying to understand the underpinnings of success.

Seth F. Hudgins, Jr.
Colonel, United States Army, Retired
President and Chief Operating Officer
U.S. Military Academy Association of Graduates

ACKNOWLEDGMENTS

I offer my unending gratitude to the United States Military Academy and to the Long Gray Line. Put bluntly, everything I am and everything I've done relates back to the Academy and to the Corps.

Many thanks to Philip DiSalvio at Seton Hall University. His regard for good schooling as it relates to good leadership—as well as the other way around—has been inspiring. Thanks also to Brian Greenstein, another great boss and advocate at Seton Hall.

I am deeply grateful to the people who brought me this project—my agent, James C. "Jimmy" Vines, and my editor, Hillel Black. Jimmy is a trusted friend and a terrific advisor who has kept this process enjoyable and rewarding. Hillel is a wonderful, patient mentor who has kept me on the right track from beginning to end.

I love and appreciate my family—Mary-Jane, Patti, and Katie—for their support and for tolerating me as deadlines approached.

And a very special thank-you to the West Point Class of 1988. Of all my accomplishments and affiliations, nothing has meant more to me than finishing the Academy with and being associated with this fine group of people. *No Task Too Great!*

INTRODUCTION

When visiting the United States Military Academy at West Point and watching a cadet parade for the first time, you cannot help but be taken aback by a setting designed specifically to inspire—and perhaps to intimidate! Four thousand young men and women, dressed in gray uniforms with polished brass, march onto a perfectly trimmed parade field. Coming to a stop before the packed bleachers, they move their rifles and sabers with a speed and precision meant to convey a message: *We are a solid, meticulous, disciplined machine.* The massive wall behind this Corps of Cadets is Washington Hall, a building of cadet barracks that—like several granite structures at West Point—looks so sturdy it appears to be cut from the rock upon which West Point sits. Toward the top of a mountain, further behind and above Washington Hall, rests the cadet chapel, yet another stone structure that looms over the proceedings as if commanding the exercise. Off to the right and below, contrasting against the hilly terrain, is the Hudson River, winding so narrowly and treacherously that there's little doubt why George Washington set up his revolutionary fortress here: a British ship would have no choice but to slow down and face the wrath of Continental Army cannons.

The setting radiates tradition, expressed in a hundred ways. The uniforms look nearly the same as they did two hundred years ago. Trains follow along both sides of the river, returning cadets from much-needed leaves, as they have for decades. And everything is decorated black, gray, and gold—the Army team colors—celebrating a college football tradition as old as the game itself.

Founded in 1802, the Academy is known for providing America with some of its most renowned leaders, including

Ulysses S. Grant, Robert E. Lee, Dwight D. Eisenhower, and Douglas MacArthur. Its graduates served in Desert Storm under the shadow of another West Pointer, H. Norman Schwarzkopf, the commander of Allied Forces in the first Gulf War. These beautiful Academy grounds are what General George S. Patton, himself a graduate, appropriately called a holy place.

Providing college and leadership education in return for military service in the United States Army, West Point has a more competitive admissions process than any other undergraduate institution in the country. Each year, nearly 14,000 high-school students apply for about one thousand cadet "appointments," leading the *Princeton Review* to label the Academy "the toughest college to get into." These applicants compete to become a part of the Long Gray Line, a lineage of great leaders who have not only won wars, but who have also gone on to build a nation. West Pointers have paved the Interstate roadways (Francis Greene) and have built the New York City railway system (Horace Porter). They have served presidents (Alexander Haig, John Block, Brent Scowcroft) and become presidents (Jefferson Davis, Ulysses S. Grant, Dwight D. Eisenhower). They have flown in space (Frank Borman, Buzz Aldrin, Michael Collins). They have headed major companies (Coca-Cola's John Hayes and Goodrich's Marshall Larsen). They have revolutionized technology and business itself (AOL founder Jim Kimsey).

The purpose of this book is to offer West Point leadership philosophies—personified by the leaders of yesterday and today—that can be applied to any management scenario. The Academy's enduring messages are meant for supervisors facing uncertain times, morality dilemmas, and team challenges. This text looks at both the Academy's institutional leadership teachings, as well as the more obscure—and, at times, humorous—

aspects of West Point life that leave its graduates ready to face life challenges in the Army, in politics, and in business.

Not every success story in this text involves a West Pointer; some simply mirror a traditional way of thinking that remains relevant in today's dynamic business world. But the focus is unmistakably on people trained at the Academy, with the hope that we all might learn from what West Point teaches its cadets—leadership concepts for work and life. Each of the book's ten chapters contains several subchapters, with topics and questions for group discussion or personal reflection following each subchapter's concise lesson.

This book considers Academy leadership training from the perspective of both the process and the person. West Point has evolved from its early 1900s history of severe plebe hazing (freshman physical abuse), and the cadets of today—with phones, computers, and liberal amounts of free time away from the Academy—undergo much less isolation than those of an earlier day. But the cornerstones of the West Point experience—the overloading of academic requirements, the existence within a self-contained military microcosm, the work duties, the unending tugging from many different directions—have endured for generations. Just as cadets discovered two hundred years ago, members of the Corps today quickly ascertain the importance of successful team dynamics ("cooperate and graduate"), that a true leader's work and turmoil, unfortunately, are never done ("it's never over"), and that leadership must therefore be taken with doses of commitment, affection, and wit ("ya gotta love it!"). The process that molds young people into West Pointers is a well-spelled-out method that is neither complex nor mystical.

However, there *is* undoubtedly an aura of mysticism surrounding the West Point personality. It is an intricate makeup of bravado, humility, risk-taking, and prescience.

It involves knowing when to push people and when to leave them to their own pace and resources, and knowing how to point them in a new, important direction. When reading any historical account of the Academy, one is presented with an assortment of personalities that make up any particular cadet class—the born leaders, the clowns, the geeks, the troublemakers, the homesick, the jocks, the collegiates. And yet, upon graduation, the commonality of traits among these new leaders is startling. Even a casual review of West Pointers throughout the generations reveals a bright, self-assured demeanor that has been contagious among their team members.

As a young brigadier general in World War I, Douglas MacArthur gained admiration among the soldiers under his command by joining them—often at length—in the gruesome trenches of no-man's-land rather than holing up with the other senior officers safely away from the battle. His confidence and words of encouragement became legend. Charles T. Menoher, the general over him, was more than impressed at the time.

> MacArthur is the bloodiest fighting man in this Army. I'm afraid we're going to lose him sometime, for there's no risk of battle that any soldier is called upon to take that he is not liable to look up and see MacArthur at his side.

MacArthur's infectious confidence would carry him and his troops through that World War, and through the next. His was a self-belief and buoyancy typical of Academy graduates then and now. It is knowledge of strategy balanced by an inclination toward impulse.

It is, quite simply, the West Point manner.

Scott Snair

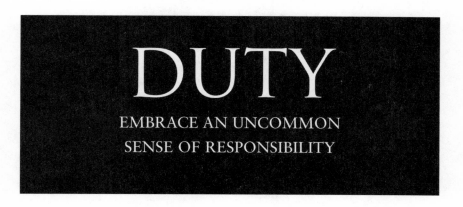

CHAPTER ONE

DUTY

EMBRACE AN UNCOMMON
SENSE OF RESPONSIBILITY

The West Pointer Asks for Responsibility

During the morning of any given July 1, about thirteen hundred young men and women hug their parents good-bye and step into the world that is West Point. The day is called Reception Day, or R-Day, and from the moment these cadet candidates come under the control of the senior-class officers, they realize that they have entered a very different world.

These young high school graduates are divided into groups and told to "report to the cadet in the red sash," who promptly reprimands them for setting down their luggage before being told to do so! A year of mind games has begun.

They are taught the position of attention, how to salute, and how to properly address anyone in sight who is not a cadet candidate.

Depending on whether or not West Point condones *pinging* during a particular year (it goes in cycles), cadet candidates are taught to *ping*—the awkward process of traveling from Point A to Point B by staring straight ahead, exaggerating one's walking pace to an odd shuffle, and staying close to the walls, particularly along hallways and when climbing or descending staircases. Pinging for the next year of one's life—now *that's* something to look forward to.

Strangely, they spend much of R-Day scooting around in white T-shirts, black gym shorts, knee-high black stretch socks and black dress shoes. In various stages and group rotations, they are given haircuts, fitted for and issued uniforms, and taught some basics about marching. A tag hangs from a pin on their shorts, indicating what stages each candidate has completed. Within several hours, all tags are fully punched.

Seek responsibility and take responsibility for your actions.

By the end of the day, wearing sharp white and gray uniforms—with the Army Band booming proudly—they march onto the parade field as the newest West Point class. They raise their right hands in unison and take an oath to defend the Constitution of the United States. Reception Day is ending and a couple of months of Cadet Basic Training, or Beast Barracks, are just getting underway.

By the time the parade has ended, several candidates have already given up and departed.

This new class marches off the parade field as "new cadets," their official title until Beast is over, when they become fourth-class cadets, or plebes.

"The entire first day is a roller coaster of emotions," says Dan Rice, a West Point graduate and currently a vice president at U.S. Trust Company of New York. "But raising your hand and taking the oath—that's when the incredible sense of responsibility kicks in. The toughest thing about plebe year is to know that, at any given time, you're free to quit and go home. You've got to want that challenge, that responsibility, early on. You've got to *ask* for it."

Rice makes an important point. The sight of R-Day mayhem generates curiosity not only because of all the oddities mentioned, but also because it involves people who are essentially *asking* for it. The beginning of such long-term, voluntary hardship runs contrary to the modern-day mentality that prefers the quick fix or the easy way out.

It almost seems outrageous that a group of young people would ask for such toil when the rest of the world is busy avoiding too much work. At most workplaces, when a tough project comes along, people scatter as if bees had been set loose amongst the cubicles. One wishes that the words "that's not my job" were just a joke phrase heard in the movies or on television. But managers hear them said daily by people at all levels within organizations.

One of the West Point Principles of Leadership—ingrained into the minds of those new cadets from the moment they set foot onto Academy grounds—is to *seek responsibility and take responsibility for your actions*. In other words, the West Pointer is part of an organization that teaches the value of looking for *more* work—work of increased volume, accountability, and dependability. A cadet's mission, simply put, is to find areas of additional responsibility.

"Taking on any tough task at work can be a lot like R-Day," says Rice. "It's stressful, fun, emotional, hilarious, tiring, and overall, unforgettable. It's the way any leader should approach a challenge."

West Pointers establish themselves as importantly unique from the outset, asking for responsibility—and all that goes with it—as if it were a reward rather than an inconvenience.

FOR CONSIDERATION:

- What is to be gained from asking for additional responsibility?

- Have you ever watched someone take on a tough task and reap the rewards for a job well done?
  What happened?

- Do people in your organization generally seek or shun responsibility? Why?

- How did volunteering ever get such a bad rap?

The West Pointer Embraces the Leader's Role

Henry did well at West Point. In fact, he finished the Academy first in his class. Following graduation, he served his country in combat as a cannon officer, was awarded the Medal of Honor, and attained the rank of lieutenant colonel at the young age of twenty-six. He gave up his officer commission ten years later and left the Army to help with the family business. He managed their shipping operations as a senior family partner and later rallied the company to restructure itself as a public corporation.

Sounds like a laudable life story. If we knew nothing else about Henry, we probably would assume from this short description that he accepted and treasured the leadership roles he was given and that he served his various teams well along the way.

Let's hear the rest of the story. Henry, it turns out, was Henry Algernon du Pont, grandson of E. I. du Pont. Following his service in the Civil War, he worked for the gunpowder company his grandfather had founded—the giant science company that today is DuPont. He also ran the Wilmington & Northern Railroad for ten years as its president. Finally, he capped his wonderful career by serving in the United States Senate for two terms.

Clearly, Henry du Pont was someone who relished the role of leader and found merit in assuming it. At any step along the way, he could have settled into his previous accomplishments, formed a routine, and relaxed—letting others take charge over the concerns of the business or the railroad or the country. Instead, he welcomed the leader's role.

Why then, so many years later, has the part of the strong leader lost favor? Leadership in many of today's organizations is a little like procreation: we innately desire it, and we need it to survive, but we are uncomfortable admitting it or discussing it freely. Indeed, many of us do all sorts of things to safely bury the concept of strong leadership in our daily business lives. We set up matrix management structures where we answer to several different bosses at once, rendering the strong leader less effective. We form work teams, committees, and subcommittees where everyone is allowed equal doses of input and everyone must be "signed on" to an idea before it goes forward. On those few occasions when we individually exercise assertive leadership decisions, we do so almost apologetically, as if we might offend people by making a decision on behalf of others and following through with it.

A company I worked for once renamed some of its front-line supervisors "resources," as if the title "supervisor" were uncomfortable for the managers or offensive to the people under their direction. Diluting or avoiding the leadership role runs contrary to even the most basic of management teachings. In their preoccupation with attempting to make everyone feel included and like an equal contributor, organizations overlook human nature and hinder themselves, spinning their teams out of control. Sure, people want to be a part of the big picture, but they also yearn for guidance, and the strong leader not only has the capacity to encourage people in the right direction, but to bring out the best in them.

The West Pointer doesn't crave power for power's sake. Instead, the West Pointer celebrates leadership as the compass that vitally guides the ship—an instrument as essential as the hull that keeps it afloat or the engine that powers it.

Instead of hiding or hampering strong leaders, companies should seek them out and celebrate them. How different a team becomes when it orbits around its leader. And how different leaders are when they sense the worth of their role and aspire to fulfill it.

As for the managers, they should not view their roles as personal burdens, embarrassments, or unnecessary impositions on others. The leader's position should instead be regarded as one intrinsically commemorated and embraced.

FOR CONSIDERATION:

- Why do people tend to avoid being in charge?

- What might be beneficial about taking on a larger leadership capacity—for you and for your team?

- What are the benefits of having a strong leader on the team? The disadvantages?

- Does your organization promote or discourage strong leaders? What can you do to further promote the role of the enthusiastic central leader?

The West Pointer Refuses to Hide
Behind Meetings and Policy

My first English professor (or "P") at the Academy was Captain Merrit Drucker, a somewhat quirky but passionate Army officer who was convinced that good grammar (like cleanliness) was next to godliness. His class topic, one day, was the "passive voice." He wanted to convince us that writing in the passive voice was not only poor grammar—it was, from a leadership perspective, copping out. That is, instead of saying, "Mistakes were made," one should be willing to say the same thing in the active voice: "I made mistakes."

"If there's one thing I hate more than anything else," he shouted at us, "it is a superior who starts a sentence with the phrase, 'It has been decided that....' It has been decided *by whom*? The world needs to know—it *demands* to know. *Who* is making this decision?"

Whew! Captain Drucker was a zealous English "P." But his point was valid. Too often we find ourselves burying our decisions and opinions within the safe haven of committee resolutions and company policies. "It has been decided that a stronger accounting of attendance is needed." Not much bite or conviction to that announcement is there? Without a boss's distinct resolve or a touch of obligatory harshness, this announcement carries with it little incentive for people to improve—to get to work on time and more regularly. How about an active voice version? "Unfortunately, due to recent absenteeism on this team, I will be paying more attention to everyone's attendance, starting tomorrow." Sounds like a firm but fair declaration from a manager clearly in charge.

Every organization has the Pious Pete, the supervisor who endlessly cites company and office policies rather than proactively owning and managing a decision. "Hey, I'm on your side," he offers insincerely to his staff. "I'd like to keep doing things the old way. But this new policy says we have to follow this new procedure." Never mind that the new procedure is better for all concerned and that Pete supported it behind closed doors. His own fears of change, of people's reactions to change, and of personal decisiveness keep Pete a busy man reciting regulations. Too bad he eventually winds up being in charge of little more than a collection of group directives and frivolous regulations.

Sure, hiding behind meetings and policies keeps us from being the bad guys. It's much easier to blame a committee meeting or some corporate directive than to own a decision—along with all the ramifications it brings to the team. No one wants to be the high school geek asking to see people's hall passes. But hey, those geeks, uh, those responsible enforcers serve a purpose. Life is not always a popularity contest. Trying to soften the blow of leadership decisions by attributing them to outside influences might keep us well-liked and accepted by the masses for another day, but it won't make us effective leaders.

Besides, who says that taking charge means being less popular? It might be a different type of popularity, but people often gravitate toward the strong-minded team leader. Studies suggest that people inherently long

Too often we find ourselves burying our decisions and opinions within the safe haven of committee resolutions and company policies.

for guidance and that they respond positively when it's offered to them. Putting your decisions out in the open and taking ownership of them before your team might not always please them, but there's a good chance that they ultimately will find your decisiveness and openness appealing, and that they will rally around you as an exceptional, willing leader.

Managers don't always go looking for ways to hide their judgment: instruments of disguise in any organization frequently make themselves readily available. One such tool is group problem-solving where everyone is responsible for a piece of the problem and follows a team script for reaching some type of consensus solution. The formula often begins with nonjudgmental brain-storming and ends, hours or days later, with a solution everyone agrees upon (at least on the surface). At the end of the process, butcher-paper sheets litter the room, smiles abound, and the charted course of action is homogeneously favored by everyone headed for the exit. Never mind that there's little ownership in such a method and little likelihood of support and success. Certainly getting input from everyone is vital to making a decision. But if the team leader is ultimately going to have to answer for the decision and the team, then it makes sense for him to direct—from the start—the decision that's going to need explaining later on.

Chuck Granitz, a forty-year veteran of General Electric and senior design engineer for GE Aircraft Engines, suggests that too often people look to meetings or policy to protect themselves. "If a manager calls a three-hour meeting about one issue, he's clearly hoping that—if a decision goes bad—he can cover his hide by explaining that everyone had ample time to screen the idea first."

Granitz says the same goes for engineers who feel obligated to stay within the comfortable parameters of previous design procedures. "Had the major computer hardware and software companies stayed within a set of design practices, we'd never have the fast-paced industry advances that are going on today. A manager should tackle the challenge of revising design policy and practices instead of following them." Granitz says that managers should not be afraid to take on bold ideas—innovative ideas that run against the grain—and own them from the start.

Captain Drucker had it right: people can use words, policies, and meetings as cover, like the concealment provided by a smoke grenade, to hide their intentions and their accountability. But such words, like the green smoke from the can, have little substance and eventually dissipate, leaving people exposed and—once hidden intentions are revealed—eventually embarrassed.

Skip the camouflage phase and go right to the point of full disclosure, out in the open, as the person in charge. Chances are you'll be filling a vacuum in your organization and carrying out a much-needed role. And you might find newfound respect and support as someone seeking team success rather than simply team popularity.

FOR CONSIDERATION:

- How often do you find yourself shrugging and saying to your team, "That's just the way things are"?

- Have you ever hidden your own directives inside the new decisions or policies of a committee? Have you ever started a sentence with, "It has been decided that…"?

- Do you hate sometimes being the "bad guy"?

- Name a recent experience where someone you knew made a tough decision and stuck with it—to the eventual benefit of the team.

- Have you ever benefited from having a take-charge supervisor?

The West Pointer Understands That Big Challenges Bring Big Gratification

John and Stuart Born are brothers and West Point graduates with a grand vision: they want to build a 300-bed, $140 million state-of-the-art hospital in an area that could benefit from the advances of today's technology-driven medicine. They have established a joint-venture agreement with a major hospital already in the region, they have rounded up investors, and they have put together a team of health-care experts, medical equipment specialists, and administrators. Now *that* is a grand challenge.

But their vision is even more impressive, almost fantastic—they want to build this hospital in Beijing, China!

Today's China is advancing economically at a rapid, admirable pace, but its health care system is lagging behind, a condition even its leaders admit to. By some accounts, the need for progress in some areas of Chinese health care is dire—a situation perhaps accentuated during the SARS outbreak in 2003. The Born brothers, from Wyoming, hope to spearhead a bold new direction in medical care. "We will provide training opportunities for doctors, nurses, and administrators in China that they have never had before," says Stuart, vice president of the project (elder brother John is the CEO). Stuart sees a day when these newly trained health care providers take their skills to parts of the country not often exposed to modern-day medicine. "We have a plan on the books to send out MDs to the rural areas to help improve health care in those areas—a MASH scenario."

Undoubtedly, John and Stuart have faced many overwhelming obstacles in realizing this dream. Early on in the process, one venture capitalist told them their mission was impossible. Too many cultural issues, regulatory issues, political barriers, and so on. Stuart says he gives a standard response: "I simply told him that this journey was going to be like my experience at Army Ranger School. Obstacles don't matter, as long as you are committed to completing the mission. You simply suck up the hardships and drive on!" And that is exactly what the Born brothers have done.

How have these two former Army officers handled the roadblocks constantly placed before them? First, they have learned how to not take no for an answer and how to always look for alternate solutions. Second, they have established a position of complete flexibility to work around obstacles and toward this lofty goal. "Our business plan has changed many times," says Stuart, "but it always has the same end state." Third, they have leaned on the individual expertise and advice of their team members. And finally, they have conducted themselves with a level of integrity so intense that everyone they deal with automatically assumes the truthfulness in their promises and projections. "We have sold our vision with very few legal documents," offers Stuart. "People know our team and the reputation of its members and they accept what we present as fact. That up-front trust has streamlined many a process."

> *Great leaders believe it is their calling—their duty—to guide their organization to a place outside its normal operating parameters and away from its comfort zone.*

The Born brothers have made a point of studying the failures of past attempts to bring Western health care to China. "Clearly, we are doing what others have tried before and failed," says Stuart. Their hope is that perseverance, savvy, and adaptability will be the formula for milestone success.

Great leaders believe it is their calling—their duty—to guide their organization to a place outside its normal operating parameters and away from its comfort zone. Taking calculated risks and a measured, well-researched series of chances, the effective leader can redefine the limits of knowledge and achievement. The grandest experiment has the potential to transform our existence.

But along with the excitement of charting new courses comes the apprehension of entering new territory. All human fears can be traced back to the one common fear—anxiety about the unknown. It is the toughest trial for the transforming leader to separate people from this inherent fear and push them forward, toward better solutions and bigger achievements. It's no wonder that the mediocre manager accepts the status quo and works to comfortably maintain it. It is far easier to keep people happy and content in their own little worlds, so that they'll make it through another workday without incident and without giving grief to the boss. The far-seeing leader looks past the immediate anguish of a challenged workforce to the magnificent improvements ahead.

Sure, taking on big challenges can bring big heartaches. But one big victory can change the world! Possessing the right attitude means visualizing the big prize.

FOR CONSIDERATION:

- When you were a kid, what grand ideas did you have about your future? Have those majestic plans become tempered over the years?

- What can be gained from maintaining a bold vision and taking on a big challenge?

- A huge challenge, admittedly, can mean a huge failure. Is it okay sometimes to make yourself and your team vulnerable to such a big fall?

- If big failures happen as the result of bold risk-taking, how can one benefit from them?

The West Pointer Is Occasionally Thrust into a Leadership Position

In the final stage of my officer training, only a few months before I would be assigned to my first Army unit, I took part in an overnight patrol exercise at Fort Sill, Oklahoma, with a group of trainees that included several close West Point colleagues. Our platoon was conducting a practice raid—an attack on an "enemy" position with the mission of destroying and then withdrawing from this mock enemy's logistics (or supply) site.

The cadre pushed us hard on this particular night as they tied together a lot of smaller lessons on combat preparation, patrolling, movement-to-contact, and night operations. The exercise was meant to be nothing less than grueling.

During the preparation and planning phase of the mission, we received a warning order on what we would be doing that night, and we were handed our individual assignments. I was delighted to be appointed as part of the rear security detail for the main body of the patrolling unit. In other words, I wouldn't have much to do. While other people were out conducting the reconnaissance of this enemy site—several miles away—or planning the attack or briefing the operation, I would be able to hang back, watch for "enemy" cadre to the rear, and essentially follow the leader into the raid. Better still, I wouldn't be under the scrutiny of the cadre. It couldn't get any easier. During the initial briefing, my eyes glazed over, complacent and convinced I wouldn't need any of the instructive information, such as the enemy situation, their suspected position, or the initial plan of attack.

I went out to the perimeter with two squad mates and manned our security position. As we surmised the recon's minipatrol would take several hours, we decided to rotate sleep, an hour for each of us.

I must have looked awfully comfortable when a cadre member approached me and tapped a stick against my helmet. "You're just the one I'm looking for," he said with a smile. "Get up and come with me." I followed the Army captain to the center of the platoon position where the platoon leader, another trainee, was marking up a plastic-coated map with a grease pencil and going over the mission plans with three of his four squad leaders, also trainees. The fourth squad leader was conducting recon.

"Guess what?" the cadre member said to the platoon leader. "You're dead. And, as the situation would have it, you just got reincarnated as rear security. Your post is that way." He pointed in the direction where he had found me.

My colleague looked bewildered for a moment, and then nodded his head. "Yes, sir." He gathered up his personal gear and his weapon, and headed for my old spot on the perimeter.

The captain then looked at me. "You're the new platoon leader. You'd better get busy on that map, and you'd better have most of your operations order written for this platoon before your reconnaissance people get back." I stared at the map and squad leaders in disbelief, feeling completely embarrassed and overwhelmed.

"Are you not up for it?" the captain asked.

I knew I was in for a miserable, challenging night, that all eyes were now on me, and that if I withdrew, I would be admitting to everyone that I was not prepared to be the new platoon leader (which, I'm sure, had been the point of the captain's placing me in that role). But I wasn't about to back down or bail out of the exercise. "I'm up for it, sir," I replied. And with that statement, I was the new leader of the platoon raid.

I set a new meeting time for thirty minutes from then, took the map, and went back to the West Point friend who had switched places with me, frankly confessing that I wasn't up on the details of the mission. He sat patiently with me on the ground and reviewed what was known at that point about the enemy, their possible position, and what he had planned to do prior to our unexpected switching of roles.

I went back to the meeting site, put together the framework for an operations order (or "OPORD") as best as I could, and briefed the squad members. Upon the return of the recon squad, we verified the existence and location of the supply depot, and changed the OPORD accordingly. The rest of the night was spent planning the platoon's movement, determining how the squads would contact and engage the enemy, how the logistics site would be destroyed, and what commands and signals would be used during each phase of the raid. We also planned how we would treat and evacuate our casualties and how we would depart once the objective had been conquered.

Be prepared for leadership—even when the need for such preparation isn't immediately evident.

Truth be told, I never fully recovered that night from the shock of being placed in charge. The plan the squad leaders and I put together was solid enough, but the planning was slow, our movement to the objective was sluggish, and we wound up attacking the mock logistics site well past the optimum time of just prior to sunrise. The enemy had the advantage of some daylight when we arrived and reacted well when they saw us coming. My self-evaluation on my performance as the redesignated platoon leader: D+.

I learned a lot that night about being prepared for leadership—even when the need for such preparation isn't immediately evident. Upon showing up for my first assignment in an

Army unit, I made a point of always knowing and understanding the mission, and understanding the bigger picture one or two levels up (if the "need to know" secrecy permitted such knowledge). I swore that never again would I find myself unexpectedly placed into a leadership role without being prepared for it. It is a philosophy I have carried with me into all aspects of management and life.

John Barry is the fraud prevention manager for all IKEA stores and operations in the United States. He notes that he has been surprised several times with new important missions or even job promotions, and he initially wonders each time if he is up to the task. "But then, I say to myself, 'Yes, I *can* do it,'" he says. "I learn as much as I can about this new mission, I tap into what is often a skilled existing team, and I charge forward."

A few years ago, Barry was handed a tough job when his company asked him to set up and take charge of a separate team that would investigate catalog-sales fraud. "It was daunting at first," he admits, "but I researched what other companies had done to thwart fraud in catalog ordering, I set up a plan, and I went to the company with it." The team that Barry helped to establish ultimately stopped 6 million dollars in 1-800 identity theft over a three-year period.

History is packed with stories about people who—in the heat of battle—find themselves thrust into leadership roles and required to make important decisions for their soldiers and the mission. It is the same with business organizations in predicaments where everyone steps back, leaving the reluctant manager still in the forefront to assume control and weather the storm. The competent manager is prepared and willing. And the inspiring leader, once placed in this unanticipated position, does not openly agonize or waffle, but instead says, "Fasten your seat belts, team, 'cause here we go!"

FOR CONSIDERATION:

- Has there ever been a situation where a leader was needed and you were hesitant to step forward? If so, why were you hesitant?

- Why is it important for an organization to have one or more members ready to assume the leader's role on a moment's notice?

- What can you do to prepare yourself for the unexpected call to lead your team?

The West Pointer Says, "No Excuse, Sir!"

It might seem odd at first glance that elite military schooling would start by teaching excuse avoidance. But that's exactly what happens at the United States Military Academy, where cadets—in the initial part of their training—are taught the merit of purging blame and excuses from their daily thoughts and conversation.

On second thought, perhaps steering clear of excuses *is* an exclusive behavior. Taking responsibility for one's situation certainly runs contrary to a modern-day culture of finding blame and embracing self-victimization. It does seem rare that we come across people who impulsively own their courses of action and accept responsibility for the positions in which they find themselves.

Early on, cadets are allowed only four responses: "Yes, sir" (or ma'am), "No, sir," "No excuse, sir," and "Sir, I do not understand." A typical "conversation" between an upperclass cadet and a new cadet might go as follows:

"Mister, do you know the second verse of 'The Star Spangled Banner'?"

"Yes ma'am."

"Begin it."

"Oh, thus be it ever when free men shall stand, between their loved homes and wild war's desolation—"

"Stop. Can you describe the Defense Meritorious Service Medal?"

(Hesitation.) "No ma'am."

"Why not, mister?"

"No excuse, ma'am."

"This time tomorrow, I want you to know your medals. Understand?"

"Yes ma'am."

The "no excuse" response is the most difficult, but perhaps most important, phrase for most new cadets to adopt. Clearly, there are many understandable reasons why this new cadet doesn't know what the Defense Meritorious Service Medal looks like. "Ma'am, I was busy last night preparing my room for inspection and I didn't have time to study my plebe knowledge." "Ma'am, our squad leader told us not to study the medals this week but to concentrate only on cadet heritage." "Ma'am, I know most of the medals, but you caught me on one I had forgotten." "Ma'am, I have a million things going on and a million things on my mind, and that medal just isn't one of them today." They are all valid excuses, but the end result in the same—he doesn't know what the medal looks like and he is supposed to know. The "no excuse" response, once embraced, puts the situation in an appropriate light. That is, the person accepts accountability for the circumstances, and, in doing so, insinuates that the problem surely is going to get fixed.

The "no excuse" response, once embraced, puts the situation in an appropriate light.

Obviously, the four allowed responses do not fit all questions posed. For example, if a new cadet is asked a question he doesn't know the answer to ("Mister, what's the top story in today's international news?"), he is not permitted to say "Sir, I do not know." That response is *not* one of four allowed responses. The new cadet is left to select an answer from an imperfect set of choices. Hmmm—an imperfect set of choices. Sounds like life—especially life as a manager—doesn't it? The goal, therefore, becomes using a limited set of choices in a somewhat satisfactory manner in responding to a limitless set of questions and problems.

When cadets first begin their journey at the Academy, they are presented with their *Bugle Notes*, a small book with much of the Army basic information and cadet lore they're initially expected to know. Many cadets have its contents ingrained before their first year is over. In *Bugle Notes*, the notion of making excuses is discussed:

> Cadets cultivate the habit of not offering excuses. There is no place in the military profession for an excuse for failure. Extenuating circumstances may be explained and submitted, but, even if accepted, such explanations are never considered excuses.

In this excerpt, the word *excuse* means a justification of forgiveness. Therefore, even if the leader is in a situation where failure is imminent and can be explained, such a predicament doesn't let the leader off the hook.

This notion brings us to an important question. When was the last time you sat in a conference room and heard someone accept full blame for a disappointing endeavor within the organization? No finger-pointing. No displays of helplessness and hopelessness. Just a clear admission of situation ownership: "Yes, I'm sorry, that was my bad decision, and I'm going to do everything I can to make it right." There is something very moving and disarming about leaders who understand the futility of extended explanation and weak rationalization, who accept and own situations—even those situations set unfairly in their laps—and go about the business of making things right.

Larry Nykwest is a technical service manager for a privately owned international paper company. He tells the story of making a decision that not everyone at his company was happy with. "Our paper had a design-related problem that made it difficult to run on the corrugating—or cardboard making— machine of one of our clients. I knew the remedy—a device on their machine that would cost about four thousand dollars. I made an on-the-spot offer to split the cost of the device with the customer. The customer agreed and installation of the device was scheduled. Unfortunately, my boss was frustrated, to say the least, with my volunteering the company to pay for half of the apparatus. At that moment, I could have made a hundred different excuses about why I felt pressured to make that offer. But I didn't. I owned up to the decision and the company paid for half of the customer's machine upgrade." Nykwest says that as he approaches twenty years in paper technical service, he would not have it any other way than to take responsibility for all of his actions.

Marketing manager Lisa Tawney Scheuerman agrees with that approach. "Excuses are like crutches," she says, "and you can never win a race if you're on crutches." People are full of excuses. Few, if any, relate to their own weaknesses. The West Point manner is an excuse-free attitude where answers and improvement are sought over pretexts, defenses, and scapegoats.

FOR CONSIDERATION:

- When was the last time you heard someone unambiguously admit to a problem without making an excuse?

- Why do we generally hate people who are full of excuses, but then tend to make excuses ourselves?

- Is there a situation in your life where forgetting about what caused the problem and taking responsibility for the outcome might make for a positive change?

- Do you think you can go an entire day without making an excuse?

West Pointers Own Their Failures

The common thread running through this chapter is ownership. West Pointers own the job of leader rather than shirking it; they own all the responsibility and decision-making that comes with the job; they own the unexpected, overwhelming challenges that sometimes come with being a leader; and they own the accountability—without excuses—that rightfully belongs to the one at helm.

But do they own failure? That is, do West Pointers occasionally admit that the challenge is over, the outcome is settled, and the goal is—sadly—not achieved? And do they personally own the failure in the same way they might have basked in the glory of success?

The answer is yes. West Pointers own their personal failures, and they take on the failures of the team as if they were personal failures.

One would imagine that an American leader such as H. Norman Schwarzkopf, a West Point graduate like his father, would neither recall nor dwell on the personal failures of his life. Indeed, one would not expect to find any flaw in the record of a four-star general who led allied forces in the liberation of Kuwait in 1991 and whose distinguished record began with an award of three Silver Star medals in the Vietnam War.

In his autobiography *It Doesn't Take a Hero*, Schwarzkopf admits to and muses on several failures during his illustrious career. For example, following his command service in Vietnam, Schwarzkopf considered working with the newly formed Training and Doctrine Command at Fort Benning, Georgia, with the promise of helping to redefine the way the new post-Vietnam Army would train and test itself. Instead, hoping to position himself for an early promotion to full colonel, he decided to pursue a high-level, high-visibility staff job at the

Pentagon. Unfortunately, the job turned out to be more politics than leadership, and Schwarzkopf missed his early promotion to full colonel. By his own admission, he failed himself in his attempt to stay ahead of the pack, and he failed the Army by turning down a position where his expertise would have benefited the most people. He writes:

> For the first time in my Army career, I'd opted for an assignment not because I wanted it, not because I felt it was where I could make the greatest contribution to the Army or my country, but because I thought it would help me get ahead. I'd decided to ticket punch.

Schwarzkopf's candor in discussing this career disappointment is telling. In owning this setback, he provides another generation of leaders with sound advice: Do what you love and what best results in good for others, and the career side of things will largely tend to itself.

Admitting ownership of one's problems benefits the team in several ways. First, acknowledging failure means the opportunity to teach others how to do better. There is no sense in asking everyone to learn by trial and error. The team can learn a great deal from the teachings of a leader who, once upon a time, did something wrong.

Second, problem ownership translates into dependability. That is, when the leader takes on ownership of a problem or a failure, others interpret this forthrightness as an assurance that the problem will be remedied. Owning a problem also introduces a time for analysis, for finding ways to ensure the mistake won't be made again. If a mistake is never owned, such an analysis never takes place, meaning the mistake is certain to be repeated.

Third, owning failure is good for the soul. It is a human acceptance of the natural tendency of life to come upon both peaks and valleys. As a leader, such peaks and valleys are often more pronounced; there are higher highs and lower lows. It is better to accept and own a valley, with the understanding that the next peak is just ahead.

> *Do what you love and what best results in good for others, and the career side of things will largely tend to itself.*

Most importantly, taking full responsibility for the team's failure sends the strong message to the team members that their leader does not intend to whitewash over mistakes and, better still, does not need a scapegoat. Such ownership often inspires the team to do better by their leader.

Every disappointment has extenuating circumstances. But West Pointers view failure as a chance to try things differently, and more intelligently, the next time around. Their admission to and possession of failure is an aspect of candor that is refreshingly distinctive, to the point of drawing admiration and inspiration.

FOR CONSIDERATION:

- What was the last failure you endured personally? Was there anything to be gained from it?

- What was the last failure your team experienced? Did you own the failure as its leader?

- What sort of message did you convey to your team following that failure? Looking back, are you satisfied with that message?

- What is the benefit of owning a failure that you didn't directly contribute to?

- Does admitting to failure hurt or help one's credibility? Does it hurt or help one's dependability?

CHAPTER TWO

HONOR

TRY SOMETHING DIFFERENT—THE TRUTH!

The West Pointer Follows an Honor Code

Not all cadets begin their Academy odyssey at West Point itself. Some candidates for admission, such as Army-enlisted soldiers who show promise for becoming officers, are sent to Fort Monmouth, New Jersey, to brush up on their math and English skills. As cadet candidates, these young people are given an extra-special and valuable preview of what they will face upon joining the Corps.

Such was the case with Mary Nagrant, a West Pointer who spent time at Fort Monmouth preparing for her cadet experience. Early on in her stay, an Army sergeant serving as a tactical non-commissioned officer (or TAC NCO) found a five-dollar bill on the floor of one of the common areas. He tacked the bill onto the main bulletin board with a note that said, "If it's yours, take it."

The bill never came down!

It remained on the board for the duration of her stay at the prep school and no one ever claimed it. "The memory of that bill up on the board stayed with me throughout my time at the Academy and to this day," she says.

Before even setting foot onto West Point grounds as a cadet, Mary learned something special about integrity: it is a virtue that is deeply inspirational, and it is very, very contagious.

Understanding the importance of being wholly truthful when caring for the lives of soldiers, Colonel Sylvanus Thayer—an early superintendent of West Point and considered the "Father of Military Academy"—established an Honor Code in the early 1800s:

A cadet will not lie, cheat, steal, or tolerate those who do.

The code is as powerful as it is simplistic. Its straightforward, unwavering nature lays the groundwork of trust and dependability upon which all good, productive things can be built. Just as computers must have the same software compatibility to communicate and assist one another, the commonality of truthfulness of all people within an organization makes for a productive exchange of ideas and a unified drive that makes great things happen.

In order to keep the Honor Code effective, cadets are taught to weigh all of their actions using the Three Rules of Thumb:

1. Does this action attempt to deceive anyone or allow anyone to be deceived?
2. Does this action gain or allow the gain of a privilege or advantage to which I or someone else would not otherwise be entitled?
3. Would I be satisfied by the outcome if I were on the receiving end of this action?

Following these rules accomplishes a lot. It ensures that not only are truthful statements being made, but that even the *perception* of misleading others, or feeling misled, is avoided. These rules reflect an appropriate "do unto others" premise that makes people feel good about their integrity efforts, that such efforts will be rewarded through the benefit of everyone else's truthfulness. Being honest about all things all the time seems, at first glance, like a tall order and largely outside the capacity of most humans. But making it happen is conceivable, and all the more so when the members of a group perceive a mutual, equally weighed benefit of reliability and believability.

Today's corporate world urgently needs but largely lacks such a functional way of thinking. Just as the value of stocks have much to do with perceptions, businesses often choose the perception of success over the reality. If balance sheets can be *made* to look solid, they are. If income statements can be *fashioned* to reflect positive profits, they do. Such surface-only whitewashing carries into the day-to-day functions of business, where people are rewarded for their performance if it is *perceived* to be useful or productive or on-message, regardless of the actual merit of their deeds. People are taught to choose a task based on how it will look on an annual evaluation form rather than what real benefit it offers them or their company.

> *Integrity: it is a virtue that is deeply inspirational, and it is very, very contagious.*

Unfortunately for pretenders, all perceptions are eventually held up against the revealing light of the truth. At some point, the Emperor's new clothes always are revealed to be nakedness. Why not make the perception match the reality in the first place?

The Honor Code is the solution—a simple system for keeping people comfortable with their trust in one another and keeping the truth at the forefront for all to see. It is a way of life that keeps an organization from being shocked and destroyed by uncovered, hidden facts. It is how all enterprises should be run.

FOR CONSIDERATION:

- Why are stories of corporate dishonesty so prevalent in today's news?

- Has it become easier or perhaps more accepted to tell untruths these days? Why or why not?

- What is the point of an Honor Code?

The West Pointer Knows MacArthur's Influence on the Honor Code

General Douglas MacArthur wasn't a part of West Point—he *was* West Point. You might argue that he still *is* West Point, as his image, his story, and his philosophies continue to filter through much of the Academy today.

MacArthur is most famous for saying "I shall return" after being ordered by President Franklin Roosevelt to depart the Bataan province of the Philippines as it was being overrun by Japanese forces during World War II. While commanding the Allied forces in the southwest Pacific, he did, indeed, return to liberate the troops who had been left behind and went on to defeat—and then to rebuild—Japan. MacArthur's highly regarded career also included commanding troops as a very young brigadier general in World War I, serving as chief of staff for the U.S. Army, and leading a United Nations force during the Korean War. He was relieved of his command by President Harry Truman for publicly arguing the need to attack China as a means of securing Korea.

Many people know that MacArthur was a West Pointer—academically ranked first in his class. Perhaps not as well known is that MacArthur served as the superintendent of West Point immediately following his service in World War I. He implemented several innovations in academics, athletics, and military training, the results of which are still being felt today.

MacArthur sought to introduce an academic curriculum that took cadets outside the box of tactics and hard sciences, striving for well-rounded leaders as officers. He saw college athletics as a vital tool for physical development and pushed for intramural and club sports programs that exist to this day. He loosened the restrictions on cadet time, allowing the Corps what was then a much more liberal leave policy to include trips into New York City, an hour's train ride away.

The general also made an important change regarding honor. When one thinks of an honor committee at any university, dark visions are conjured up of dungeon-like rooms with solemn young men in black hoods reading by candlelight as they pour over old decrees written on yellowing parchment.

Just as duplicity breeds duplicity, openness breeds openness.

Perhaps, in a sense, such was the case at West Point, where honor initially had been enforced clandestinely by the cadets themselves. Rather than having an honor offender officially expelled from the Academy, cadets would "silence" the culprit or make things so miserable for him that he would leave on his own. MacArthur, in 1916, discovered that such a stealth organization existed within the Corps. Rather than seeking to abolish it, he took the surprising step of officially recognizing it—putting it on the books and creating a formal honor committee with regulations—with the hope of bringing honor enforcement out of the shadows into open discussion and into the sanctioned development of young people's characters. Thus, the honor system was officially recognized by the Academy.

MacArthur understood that, when it comes to codes and standards, the effective leader creates an environment where issues are debated and decisions are reached in the light of day, making organizational understanding, acceptance, and enforcement easier. Such actions foster a setting where people are less inclined to keep secrets, creating fewer instances where such secrets might be hidden under lies and half-truths. Just as duplicity breeds duplicity, openness breeds openness.

This young, thirty-six-year-old superintendent also appreciated that policies of character are better implemented when they have a human face to them—the face of the team leader. By making the honor system and its regulation official, he made himself the visible, flesh-and-blood center of focus for the system. Although the Corps still "owned" the Code, it now had the appropriate influence and advice of a senior officer necessary to make it a teaching vehicle, and it had the capacity to pull the set of rules out of the dimness and into the light of lively, productive discussion.

MacArthur's innovations were not, by any means, greeted with open arms. Stubborn faculty (some of whom had been around when *he* was a cadet) and hostile old graduates fought what they perceived to be a softening of the Academy, particularly when MacArthur sought a more flexible academic curriculum with choices and elective courses. Such obstinacy continues today, as most graduates are convinced the Corps went to hell the day after their graduation and don't mind complaining to the superintendent about any proposed change they have caught wind of. That MacArthur was able to push as much of his vision past such walls of resistance serves as testament to his convictions.

After publishing my first business book in 2003, I floated an idea to my agent for a second book: a business parable, telling the story of MacArthur in the late 1950s encountering a time traveler from the future. In my story, MacArthur is transported to the new millennium, takes charge of a large corporation, and—using basic tenets of integrity, influence, and strategic ingenuity—saves it from the deceptive accounting practices that would have made it collapse (and, in the real world, *did* make it collapse). Unfortunately, my agent suggested there wouldn't be much of a market for such a book. Why? Because with so many giant corporations crumbling under the weakness of their balance-sheet gamesmanship, the story had essentially become old news. That is, when one company deceives us, gets caught, and has their stock value plummet, the story is current and interesting—book-worthy, shall we say. But when such a phenomenon happens repeatedly, the effect is numbing. In my parable, MacArthur would have to teleport to so many different companies in order to save American faith in the market, the story would become, well, a little too far-fetched!

FOR CONSIDERATION:

- Does honesty within an organization come easier when there is a strong, example-setting leader to rally around?

- Might integrity issues be more easily dealt with if done so openly, according to a set of straightforward procedures?

- How might you go about formalizing integrity policies and procedures in your organization?

The West Pointer Understands
the Challenged Corporate Leader

In spite of example after example of business trickery ultimately exposed, managers seem more inclined to deceive than ever. It looks as if today's corporate leaders are challenged and pressured on so many levels and in so many different ways that the urge to take integrity short cuts is overwhelming. Furthermore, due to the watering down of influential leadership in today's managerial models, bosses are less influential but every bit as answerable for the results of these concerns. How do they fill the gap? Often with the hastily improvised putty of truth manipulation or fact fabrication.

When such forgery and falsehood begin to seem like the hidden norm rather than the unfortunate exception, we all tend to lose faith. A time traveler from a few decades ago, like MacArthur, journeying into the today's business world undoubtedly would be shocked and deeply disheartened by the extent of today's high-profile corporate scandals.

For example, what could be more clearly egregious than issuing false profit statements? One would think that documents issued to stockholders and potential stockholders were so sacred and so scrutinized that no one would consider playing games with them. And yet, inflating profits on an income statement has been one of the more common ploys in this labyrinth of corporate deceit. Such deception includes hiding losses through perplexing partnerships or lying about the number of recurring customers. Some companies have been caught trading accounts with each other, with no hard currency changing hands, attempting to make business look brisker than it is. The Enron, WorldCom, and Global Crossing stories have become so commonplace in the newspapers that one becomes numb to the modern-day ethical tragedy they represent.

Such scandals have carried over to the auditors responsible for authenticating the accuracy of a company's books. Hungry for lucrative consulting work, some accounting firms have willingly massaged numbers. Instead of acting as objective overseers of statistics, they have been exposed as accessories to the treachery. It is stunning, for example, how a reputable accounting firm such as Andersen could implode so quickly under a scandal of questionable audits and destroyed documents.

Investment analysts have joined in the betrayal, offering overly optimistic stock reviews to the public, hoping to gain banking business (and pay bonuses) from the companies benefiting from their generous "buy this stock" recommendations.

The eternal optimist might think these transgressions were the actions of wayward underlings and that the noble, upright senior leadership had no idea what was going on. Surely such an optimist would be rendering this judgment from a secluded island. The behavior of those at the top of the food chain suggests not only culpability, but perhaps even some one-upmanship. Various criminal and regulatory investigations of CEOs have revealed tax evasion, the use of enormous and improper expense accounts, and the paying of unauthorized fees to friends. CEOs have been caught borrowing excessive amounts from their companies to purchase shares at misguidedly inflated prices. They have even been accused of crimes as basic as looting the company vaults!

Such prevalent displays of dishonesty have made us not only doubt the integrity of those we trusted to build and run our systems of commerce, but also question the basic notion that many free societies are built upon: that people, left to themselves, will start businesses that fill a public demand and will grow those businesses within legally set boundaries to benefit *both* themselves and the general populace. When the common good of the company or the population appears to be removed from the leadership's compass, people's confidence in the marketplace ceases to be a driving economic force.

As an advocate for raw honesty, the West Pointer might be expected to look down upon this corrupt mess from a lofty granite temple. To the contrary, the West Pointer understands the mentality of the tested corporate leader more than anyone. Army officers on all levels—some managing groups of people larger than the largest conglomerate—are under enormous pressure to convey success to their superiors throughout a wide range of ever-changing responsibilities. The impulse to fudge a seemingly minor status report in order to concentrate on a more important matter is always there. A must-win, accept-no-errors culture intensifies the urge.

Rather than looking down on human limitations, effective leaders accept them and learn from them, seeking to appreciate the circumstances that have destroyed many a corporate icon.

The West Pointer learns as a freshman, or "plebe," about the natural desire to lie. Approached endlessly with questions and directions from upperclass cadets, the plebe is expected to occasionally blurt out an untruth—instinctively yearning, for a split second, to satisfy a higher-ranking cadet with a misleading answer. Such an answer is called a "pop-off response." The plebe is allowed, on the spot, to correct the statement without fear of Honor Code repercussions. The Academy not only understands the inherent desire to fib; it also recognizes that immediately rectifying such an action keeps the betrayal from snowballing—to the tune of, say, several billion dollars.

Like West Point, businesses can set up candid environments where financial transactions and corporate decisions are revealed unashamedly for all to review. Alan Fazzari is the vice president of people services, quality-control processes, and technology for a mid-sized electronics manufacturer in New Jersey. He suggests that his company atmosphere is "a fertile ground for ethical behavior" because of its aggressive, full-view decision-making and open-door policies. "Everything's out in the open," he says, "to the point where anyone can question an act that doesn't immediately seem right."

As does West Point, Fazzari advocates preventive rather than reactionary ethical training. "The up-front money we spend on ethics training is well invested, considering the cost of having to react to questionable deeds."

Rather than looking down on human limitations, effective leaders accept them and learn from them, seeking to appreciate the circumstances that have destroyed many a corporate icon. After all, clear understanding translates into educated prevention. The effective manager is realistic about human frailties while aggressively seeking to be good-hearted and honorable.

FOR CONSIDERATION:

- Why are managers under such pressure to "alter" the truth?

- Why do managers continue to lie in spite of the increasing number of people getting caught?

- Why do people seem conditioned to tell untruths? Is it possible to fight this innate urge?

- Does the integrity climate of an organization help the team leader to stay the course of uprightness? If so, how?

West Pointer Files Anecdotes of Integrity

The West Pointer understands that there's no reason to re-invent the wheel. At the Academy, there are shelves of case studies that describe cadets being placed in situations where their integrity is challenged. Life and morality rarely present themselves in delineations of black and white, and a cadet often finds himself in areas of gray where the right course of action is still expected and the honor system is no more for-giving. The solution is to look at archives of past dilemmas and model one's behavior after the debated and approved actions of past cadets.

When I was a cadet, we had location placards outside our rooms—signs with markers indicating where we were at any given time. Each cadet was responsible for marking his or her card before heading to any particular destination. The placards clearly were meant to keep track of cadets and prevent them from sneaking off the installation for prohibited fun and frivol-ity. The cards were also a source of anguish for cadets who wanted to be truthful in their words, but perhaps a little playful in their actions. Mischievous but concerned cadets wondered where disregard for regulations merged with dishonorable behavior or untruthful statements.

By checking the case-study binders, roguish cadets found the solution: they could mark their cards under the category *Unmarked*, meaning "No statement." By not stating one's whereabouts on the location placard, a cadet essentially was not making a statement and, therefore, not telling a lie. If caught, a cadet would be punished, but not expelled for dis-honorable conduct. Such research came in handy each year when a stealthy group of cadets snuck off to Maryland to cap-ture and hold hostage the U.S. Naval Academy mascots—goats with their horns painted blue.

On the serious side, the case studies involved more sober scenarios, such as how to properly document other people's work when writing a research paper or how cadets were to handle themselves when they saw other people committing crimes or honor violations. In most cases, the case studies indicated that cadets were obligated to report infractions they witnessed.

The use of such case studies carries over nicely into military service, where young officers are handed scenarios during their basic course and eval-

The goal is to benefit from the experiences of others and the quandaries others have had to face.

uated on how they react. Often, such testing is based on real-life settings, and the performance of the officer in the simulation is weighed against real-life decisions. Again, the goal is to benefit from the experiences of others and the quandaries others have had to face.

The tracking and recording of integrity situations can work effectively in the business world as well. If nothing else good ever comes from the earthshaking corporate scandals that rocked the United States at the beginning of the millennium, the documentation and study of how so many things went so terribly wrong might set the learning in motion for a new philosophy—a new, honorable course.

At a paper mill where I used to work, the weekend management team once anguished over whether or not a new additive fell within the specifications of one of our most important customers. A huge shipment of the chemical had just been delivered, a product that helped the mill with all sorts of strength requirements. The weekend team wanted to use it upon delivery. Unfortunately, it was a holiday weekend, and the people most familiar with the additive were not answering their home phones.

The shift supervisor, the smallest fish in the managerial food chain, walked into the conversation. "Check the logs," he said matter-of-factly.

Everyone stared at him. He continued. "I'm sure we were running this type of paper when we ran the trial for that new additive a month or so ago. See what the customer had to say back then."

The old foreman logbooks were kept in a closet just to the rear of the conference room. The weekend team quickly found the journal entries for the week when the new chemical was trialed. It turned out that this customer's product *had* been produced with this chemical and that a few sheets rushed to the customer had been approved. The decision to use the additive was easy at that point.

What might have happened without that record? Who knows? In a pinch to have a productive weekend, the team might have turned their uncertainty into a deception, using the chemical without openly documenting it and, upon finding out the customer hadn't approved its use (in cardboard boxes), facing yet another morality decision of continuing the deception or coming clean. By accessing a document clearly stating what a previous team had done and what the customer's reaction had been, the weekend team was given an appropriate path to follow.

Keeping records can be done on a very personal level, as a leader seeks to benefit from her past actions and the experiences of others she has observed. What she will probably find is that unethical decisions—or situations that lend themselves toward unethical decision-making—can be categorized. The circumstances that make us want to lie or cheat have a lot to do with how our human minds instinctively perceive a situation. When chronicled, they tend to fall under a few discernible groups.

First, there are situations involving peer pressure. People feel a strong, innate pressure to be acknowledged and accepted by those around them—including their boss, their coworkers, and the people they manage. The easiest way to garner such acceptance is to say the things these people want to hear and do the things they would like to see happen. Don't ever convince yourself that peer pressure ended with high school. The desire for peer acceptance is a fierce form of repression, not easily conquered, and which sets the stage for much of today's dishonesty.

Second, there are situations involving all-or-nothing assessing. That is, some people and organizations seek error-free performance, ignoring the notion that there is much knowledge to be gained by learning from mistakes. The Army historically has struggled with such burdensome attitudes, where soldiers and officers are afraid to share shortcomings or admit oversights. Fortunately, the military culture has made tremendous gains against this condition, becoming more open about errors and failings in the hope of obtaining advice and the shared experiences of others who've "been there."

Third, there are situations involving needless prophecy. That is, we anticipate the worst possible scenario if we admit the truth or follow the "harder right." So we choose to lie or travel the unfortunate path of least resistance, avoiding horrible repercussions that, in all likelihood, never would have happened (or at least would not have been so formidable).

It is possible to react appropriately to integrity dilemmas at work. One simply needs to keep a personal record of past moral challenges and how they were successfully managed.

FOR CONSIDERATION:

- Have you ever made a decision based on the documented actions of another person in a similar situation? Were you the one who had written or filed that document?

- What might be the benefits of you or your team starting a file on issues and situations, especially those related to integrity?

- Has peer pressure ever pushed you toward a less-than-honest action?

- Does an everything-perfect attitude in your organization sometimes push people to whitewash results?

- Has excessive fear of the future ever induced you to lie?

The West Pointer Welcomes
the Paradoxically Freeing Nature of Honesty

Mary Nagrant, who watched the five dollar bill stay untouched, understands how the Honor Code can serve as a lighthouse on a rocky beach. After her time in the Army, she went to work as a logistics planner for a large company. On several occasions, it was suggested to Nagrant that she should, well, be creative with some ledger entries in order to help her site meet its goals on paper. She repeatedly refused. Was Nagrant rewarded or openly complimented for the stand she took? Did people rally around her as an example? Hardly. "My performance reviews suggested that I wasn't able to make numbers work," she says. "The pressure to play games with the figures was always there." She subsequently got out of logistics planning rather than give in to the coercion.

Curt Herrick is a West Pointer who works as an operations manager in the e-sales and services division of a giant telecommunications company. He was faced with a similar experience when he first joined the company as a front-line supervisor for a team of ten repair technicians. The techs all had company cars for making repair calls "in the field." Herrick soon realized that because of changing technology, his team's work was becoming confined to a few company buildings, entailing desktop computer, network, and network server repairs. In sum, the cars were no longer needed. His workers were not leaving their homes to go to repair jobs. They were using company cars simply to drive back and forth to work each day. The Rules of Thumb suggested that they had gained an unfair advantage over other workers at the expense of the company. Herrick felt it appropriate to have the cars taken away.

Did people willingly go along with his rationale and respect him for reallocating the company's resources appropriately?

No. In fact, all hell broke loose. "A firestorm of complaints and grievances set in," he says. "They had come to view those cars as an entitlement." Making matters worse, Herrick's recommendation drew attention to a few managers who still retained the cars they had used as technicians. He found one manager's rationale particularly disheartening. "Her logic," he says, "was that the lease was costing the company only twenty dollars a month." The notion that the company was not benefiting from this expense either didn't occur to her or didn't have an impact on her. As cars were taken away, Herrick felt the resentment toward him. "They figured I was just bucking for promotion" rather than just doing the right thing, he says.

Upon reading these stories, one cannot help asking, "Hey, where's the happy ending?" Was Mary Nagrant invited back as a planner with a big promotion once the company realized the error of its ways? Did Curt Herrick's team approach him at

West Point teaches this concept as choosing "the harder right over the easier wrong," meaning that people frequently do not respond well to actions of pure integrity.

some point with a group apology and offer him their everlasting loyalty? No. On the contrary, in both cases, doing the right thing was "rewarded" with condemnation, unofficial censure, and more heartache. The easier course, in both scenarios, would have been to give people what they were asking for, regardless of the ethics. Following a personal code of honor rarely makes the people around you happy. West Point teaches this concept as choosing "the harder right over the easier wrong," meaning that people frequently do not respond well to actions of pure integrity around them.

So why push so hard for the truth when it usually gets you grief? The answer has two parts. First, choosing to say and do ethical things—rather than the things people want to hear and see—means that you reap the benefits of a *pay me now or pay me later* philosophy. A lie very often comes back to haunt you later on, in magnified form. The end result is accusation, criticism, and embarrassment much worse than anything that could have come from doing the appropriate, truthful thing in the first place. Taking the up-front antagonism and persecution from people who can't handle the truth means not having to deal with much worse later on. For example, Herrick's supervisor knew about the tough course he was taking and ultimately commended him for it.

Second, being less than truthful is addictive. Lies and less-than-moral actions usually lead to more lies and less-than-moral actions, often in heightening degrees. Some of this behavior happens to cover up previous activities. But other times, people get so used to offering lies that they grow into a habit of it, a numbness that hides the increasing impact of the fabrications. It's like any other addiction, where small doses don't get you the same results they used to, so you choose larger doses for the same payoff. Choosing the truth from the start means saying no to the addiction of dishonesty.

The result of prevalent organizational lying is a labyrinth of deceit that can be difficult to see through. West Pointers use the undiluted truth as the beacon that guides them out of this maze and into the calming light of uprightness. That's the paradoxically freeing nature of honesty. Instead of choosing the appropriate mix of lies and truths that will keep you, your boss, and your team happy, you free yourself from future anguish and take the path of integrity. If it ultimately means breaking away from an organization that doesn't do business honestly, then you're free from the corruption that most assuredly would have hobbled you later on. If it means enduring the immediate disdain from those who desire the status quo of white lies and hidden ways of doing things, then you're free to push on to bigger goals for you and your organization, unhampered by the shackles of small minds.

The athlete's creed, "No pain, no gain" applies to the Honor Code as well. The initial pain of choosing the "harder right" means gaining future advantage over others who prefer to work in the shadows. Lies don't get you things—truths do.

One final thought on the people who initially resist your attempts at truthfulness: Invariably, people are asked for feedback on the successful leaders in their organization. A typical question: "What is it about this manager that you like the most?" What is the response you're most likely to hear? "I like him because he tells it like it is." Such a compliment may very well come from a coworker who resisted that manager's earlier efforts at making wrong things right.

The path of honesty, while not the easiest one to walk, does—in the long-term—offer you the most freedom, the least amount of overall hardship, and the ultimate respect you need from people to make wonderful things happen.

FOR CONSIDERATION:

- Has there been a situation in your organization where choosing the white lie would have saved you all sorts of grief? What did you do?

- Is there a difference between what people want to hear and what they *think* they want to hear? If so, why is it important for a supervisor to understand the difference?

- How does choosing the truth "free" you as a manager?

The West Pointer Realizes That Morality Challenges Are Nothing New

You could argue that people change. You also could argue that times change, but people don't. Which is more accurate? There is good reasoning for either claim. Certainly, people have grown more enlightened over the generations, as volumes of teachings and information have become more widely and easily available. On the other hand, you can't help but notice the similarities between the dilemmas we are faced with today and those faced by people two years ago, two hundred years ago, or two thousand years ago. Hoping to gather lessons from the lives and happenings of the past is a noble aim. After all, there's no sense in turning your back to history. Appropriately, the West Pointer studies up on the rich chronicles of honor challenges—military, political, and corporate—seeking to learn from them and avoid falling victim to a similar, modern-day hazard.

For example, as a cadet, I studied the integrity challenges the Army was confronted with in the 1980s as it made decisions about the M247 Division Air Defense (DIVAD) gun, also known as The Sergeant York. The weapon was an anti-aircraft gun and a radar-tracking system, all set on the turret of a tracked vehicle. Its design and production had been accelerated, and the Army essentially had been given carte blanche to make it happen. Without the normal oversight of most weapon design and production, the Army had pushed the project forward in spite of several red flags. The radar could not track aircraft flying very low or very high. The turret could not traverse fast enough for the gun to track a fast-moving aircraft. The vehicle moved too slowly to travel with the tracked vehicles it had been designed to protect, such as the M1 Abrams tank. In short, the project was a disaster, and yet onward it went. Only after several dozen vehicles were produced, at a cost of $6 billion dollars, did the project finally get appropriately scrapped. Clearly, people along the way—intelligent people who knew the project had become a worthless mess—had felt the pressure to continue instead of speaking up. It is a wonder, looking back, that the project got canceled at all.

The West Pointer also looks outside the military and considers integrity failings in the world of politics. One certainly doesn't have to look far, as the

Studying the history of ethical predicaments can help prevent morality challenges.

phrase "honest politician" now sounds like a contradiction in terms. But if one considers unscrupulous behavior to be the norm in politics, then viewing political history from a perspective of disdain and wonderment is instructive and good for the leader's soul. Perhaps the most glaring example of ethically challenged political leadership is the Nixon presidency, where Richard Nixon and his tight-knit group of partisans put together lists of enemies and connived ways to foil them. The group's attempt to cover up the breaking and entering of the Democratic National Committee Headquarters at the Watergate Hotel during Nixon's re-election campaign in 1972 was its undoing. Again, lies were used to cover lies, until an appalled nation forced Nixon to resign. Many have since speculated, in one form or another, how much political damage might have been averted had Nixon and his team simply acknowledged their underhanded strategizing early on and placed themselves at the mercy of the public. Considering the political damage, the prison sentences, the ruined lives, and the shame and disillusionment of a nation, coming clean at any point undoubtedly would have been the wiser move.

As for what's currently going on in the corporate world, the West Pointer is faced with an endless list of cases to consider. The problem is not which occurrences to examine, but rather it is how to categorize them and make sense of them. Aiming to produce well-rounded leaders, the Academy wants cadets to understand the culture of business, what makes it work, and what makes it susceptible to corrupt influences. After all, soldiers don't build weapons; civilian corporations build them. The ill-conceived process that produces an ineffective air-defense weapon involves a series of problems to be addressed from the military angle *and* from accounting, financial, statistical, and logistical perspectives. It is wise to consider corporate ethical dilemmas in groups. First, there is theft—stealing or misappropriating corporate funds or assets. Second, there is the group of brazen paper offenses, such as issuing false profit statements or misrepresenting company liabilities. Third, there is the category of "turn a blind eye" offenses, such as glossing over the presumed accuracy of accounting statements.

The fourth group of misdeeds the West Pointer must consider is the transgressions that fall within the gray area. For example, when does portraying a company's stock as strong leave the definition of pro-company optimism and enter the realm of deception? When does tax planning become tax evasion? The answers are not always apparent, as the boundaries are not easily defined.

In the previous chapter, I mentioned technical service manager Larry Nykwest, who was criticized by his company management for offering to pay for half of a customer's machine upgrade. He fully understands the ethical pressure placed on business supervisors who have to make quick decisions and are then faced with having to own up to them. "When I realized that I had made a choice that might not be well received by my boss, I easily could have hidden that upgrade expense in my customer return ledger," he offers. "Instead, I took the high road and faced the initial wrath my admission created." Nykwest suggests that choosing to hide mistakes—even the smallest ones—

comes back to haunt all managers, including the ones who think they have been clever in covering their tracks.

The team leader takes solace in the fact that these challenges are nothing new, that they have been around in one form or another for centuries, and that studying the history of ethical predicaments can help prevent them.

During the study of ethical histories, the West Pointer finds a constant. Just as the U.S. Constitution offers continuity throughout the changes of generations (changes that seem to be accelerating), the Honor Code is meant to serve as the norm. It is the thread of stability that weaves itself through the ever-changing array of ethical trials.

FOR CONSIDERATION:

- Historically, what have been the ethical challenges facing your particular profession?

- Have these challenges changed over the years, or have they remained consistent?

- What benefit is to be gained from knowing that similar types of integrity challenges have been faced by different people over many generations?

- Can a set of integrity standards be established that will carry your organization through a variety of different and ever-changing scenarios?

The West Pointer Endures Some Weakness, But Seeks Faultlessness

Throughout the discussion of honor and the study of ethical dilemmas, West Pointers set themselves apart from others in a big way. While accepting and addressing human frailties, West Pointers seek the seemingly unreachable ideal. They *believe* in the notion of a completely truthful soldier. They *trust* the concept of the honest politician. They *have faith in* the ability of businesspeople to clean up their acts and seek profit fairly. The purpose of considering the moral failures of others is not to point the finger, but to find ways to maneuver through one's own ethical trials.

Successful leaders never shrug their shoulders and say, "*Everybody* does it." They hold on to the possibility that a workplace can exist where everybody doesn't do it and perhaps where *no one* does it—where people live and work in an environment of openness and dependability and aren't forever scrutinizing the claims of others, looking for the untold story, or fishing for hidden meanings. Good leaders not only strive for integrity, they strive for honest internal debate and the self-policing that comes with it.

With any business plan, wishing to maintain a status quo is foolish. Situations rarely stay the same; at any given time, they are either getting better or worse. Such is the integrity position of an organization.

What makes great leaders different? They hold ideals. Instead of giving in to cynicism, they follow models and principles, stretching for that unreachable ideal. They're never satisfied with "pretty honest" or "generally reliable." They seek unrefined integrity, perfect behavior, and the great results that surely must come with them.

I once lamented to a mentor of mine how demanding my bosses were. Having recently taken over a production team

that, by all accounts, had its problems, I was hoping the expectations would be low. Certainly, I would have been able to meet
or exceed low expectations. But I had entered a job with high
expectations, and I often had a lot of explaining to do about
why the standards were not being met.

"How am I supposed to get these things done," I asked. "I
would have to be able to fly in order to make them happy."

"Well then," offered the mentor, "it's time you grew some
wings."

I saw his point. My
objective needed to be
meeting the high expecta-
tions and not feeling vic-
timized or overburdened.
And, in the end, he was
right. Although I eventu-
ally understood that peo-
ple were being more
patient than I had imagined, striving for the lofty goals my
bosses had set meant thinking and acting productively as I
stretched for that unreachable ideal. In the end, I appreciated
and benefited from the challenge. Such is the case with integrity,
where we never want people to be satisfied with anything less
than an ideal. Desiring such heights, as said before, has a tendency to be contagious.

What makes great leaders different? They hold ideals. While accepting and addressing human frailties, great leaders seek the seemingly unreachable ideal.

While the Honor Code is absolute in its expectations (and, at
the Academy, in its enforcement), the teachings stemming from
it are based on the concept of less-than-perfect people aiming for
near-perfect uprightness and reliability. Grounded in the workplace reality of human frailty and failings, the West Pointer still
seeks precision and excellence from those on the team.

FOR CONSIDERATION:

- Does it make sense to have a goal that might never be reached?

- Although honesty, in its pure definition, shouldn't have varying degrees, is it possible, in a practical sense, to be "less honest" or "more honest"?

- Is it possible to improve at being honest?

- Has there ever been a time when you accepted a weakness in someone while swaying them toward stronger behavior?

CHAPTER THREE

COUNTRY

BE A PART OF SOMETHING
BIGGER THAN YOU

The West Pointer Senses the Intrinsic Need to Devote Oneself

Cadets don't always enter West Point as impassioned patriots. That is, patriotism isn't always their primary reason for attending the Academy. The need for challenge, the aspiration for self-improvement, the hope of attending a top-notch college, the desire to please one's parents (many of whom are graduates themselves)—these factors often dominate at the outset of a cadet's career. Truth be told, for any skeptical young man or woman, passionate adoration for one's country might initially seem like an old person's trait. Furthermore, education at West Point does not include the type of red-white-and-blue indoctrination one might expect from a military academy. To the contrary, cadets are taught American history in an inquisitive, probing—even critical—fashion, following the belief that loyalty is most valuable when it is not blind, and that when people are devoted to an establishment in spite of its flaws, their devotion is often matched with a talent and desire to help correct those flaws.

But if cadets don't arrive at the Academy with patriotism in their blood, they invariably graduate with a love of country in their hearts. Having taken courses over the years like "History of the Military Profession," they have learned about the battles fought, the sacrifices made, the convictions felt, and the challenges met throughout the history of the United States. West Pointers depart their alma mater with a profound desire to help write a story that was started over two hundred years ago—a story with continuous themes, maxims, and traditions. They feel obligated to build on a way of life that began generations before and to set the stage constructively for their successors.

Loyalty is most valuable when it is not blind.

To the casual observer, patriotism might not be so easily linked with leadership. Surely someone can be an effective manager without being a committed flag-waver. And—appreciating the allegory—a person can be a good boss within an organization without having to *love* the organization. However, there is an important difference between love and loyalty. The truly effective leader is loyal to the organization— but, again, not blindly loyal. Loyalty without scrutiny isn't good for anyone—not for the leader, not for members of the organization, and not for the organization itself. But being loyal, while respectfully inquiring about an organization's direction and its means for getting there, is beneficial to all concerned. The dedicated manager can be counted on to help set the right course for the team, rather than tagging along like an eager puppy.

Successful leaders understand not only the importance of being openly committed to a team and its causes, but also the intrinsic need of human beings to devote themselves. There-fore, if the *leader* expresses devotion, there's a strong likeli-hood the team will follow suit and become devoted as well. West Point cadets are taught about Abraham Maslow, a pio-neer of humanist psychology in the 1940s and 1950s. Maslow's still-famous "Hierarchy of Needs" suggests that people want to belong to a team, devote themselves to a team, and be accepted by that team more than anything other than the most basic human physical needs. The need to belong and to devote ourselves is a powerful part of what makes us people, and it is an aspect of human nature that the effective leader comprehends and utilizes to the advantage of the team.

Keep in mind that devotion to one's cause or institution doesn't always lead to the neatly wrapped happy ending. In fact, such dedication can be an agonizing endeavor. Cadets at West Point are taught about the Academy's role in the U.S. Civil War, when about a thousand West Pointers were asked to choose their personal allegiances to either the Union or the Confederacy. In the end, the overwhelming majority of gradu-ates chose to side with their home states. In nearly every major battle of the Civil War, the armies on both sides were com-manded by West Pointers.

Importantly, cadets are taught about Civil War era graduates who broke the norm and chose sides based on conviction rather on geography. For example, one of only a few dozen Southern graduates to side with the North was Robert Anderson. Born in Kentucky, Anderson felt strong ties to the South and to his fam-ily. But Anderson, like all Army officers, had sworn an oath to defend the United States, and his dedication to and interpreta-tion of that oath prompted him to reject secessionism. He decided to fight to keep the country whole.

During the war, Anderson was given the tough task of commanding the forts occupied by Union forces in Charleston Harbor, South Carolina. Among them was Fort Sumter, a prime target of Confederate forces. He refused to give up Sumter until it was bombed to rubble and splinters. And when Confederate troops stopped firing long enough to allow him to surrender the post, Anderson marched out with his troops, drums playing and the Union colors flying. Now *that's* devotion!

Patriotism can be superficial. The love of country a West Pointer feels goes deeper, relating to more than just a flag. It suggests a profound devotion to cause and principle.

FOR CONSIDERATION:

- Why is it an inborn quality of people to immerse themselves in a belief, an institution, or a cause?

- How does a deep awareness of devotion make someone a better manager?

- Is it likely that such dedication is contagious? How might it affect other members of the team?

The West Pointer Sees Country as Belonging

West Point graduate Jeff Keen is an administrator at the Office of Federal Housing Enterprise Oversight in Washington, D.C. His job entails monitoring the security and financial soundness of government-sponsored enterprises such as Fannie Mae and Freddie Mac. Keen finds working in the nation's capital rewarding and inspiring. "I look out of my office window each morning and see the Executive Office Building," he says. "It reminds me of the important decisions being made around here every day. It's very moving."

Keen remembers a turning point in his life when the concept of *country* became more personal—more related to people. As a young cadet in the 1980s, he was completing the Basic Airborne Course ("Jump School") at the U.S. Army Infantry School in Fort Benning, Georgia. The course concluded with five different parachute drops on different days from a C-130 aircraft. The jumps included parachute-only jumps with no equipment ("Hollywood jumps"), jumps with full-combat gear, and tactical jumps at night. The parachutes were deployed by static lines, meaning that all the would-be paratroopers had to do was step out the door and their chutes would open in seconds. During the required night jump, Keen was comfortably in the middle of a line of trainees ready to go. Being in the middle of the pack was easiest on the nerves.

"Being towards the back of the line made things too easy for someone to step aside if the fear took him over," he observes. "Being towards the front of the line meant being able to see outside, and that was tough on the courage as well."

Keen meant that looking out into the uncertain darkness of night didn't make things any easier for the people up front. Standing sandwiched in the middle of the pack gave him some comfort that the flow of people in front of him and behind him would be adequate to overcome his intense fear to leave the plane—a fear that had gotten worse, not better, with each jump. *If all of your friends jumped off a bridge, would you go jumping too?* Well, sure, if half of them were in front of you leading the way and half of them were behind you shoving you toward the edge!

On the command of the jumpmaster, as the airplane crossed over the drop zone, the line moved briskly, as students jumped quickly and successively out the door. Keen advanced rapidly toward the door, knowing his fear was about to be over—once outside the door, the airborne trainee had nothing to do but check the canopy, feel the rush of adrenaline, and enjoy the ride down to earth.

That's when the arm came up.

Keen bumped into the arm. "Stop!" shouted the jumpmaster. "We're coming around again! You'll go out on the next pass!" Keen was now the first in line for the next pass over the drop zone, and all the terror of what was outside the plane— the cold air, the pitch black, an awareness of the speed they were traveling—was right in front of him. After the plane completed a few banks, the jumpmaster looked at Keen. "You— stand in the door!"

Keen hesitated, and then positioned himself with his hands holding the sides of the open aircraft door, the wind pushing hard against him. There was nothing to see below but darkness—like the blackness of a bottomless abyss. The jumpmaster, sensing his fear, leaned toward Keen, smiling. "Pretty damned scary, ain't it?"

"In all honesty," says Keen, recalling the moment, "I came as close to stepping aside and washing out of the course as a person can get without actually doing it."

So what kept him from stepping aside? "I looked back at the fellow trainees behind me," Keen says. "At that moment, I felt more a part of a group than I've ever felt before. And thinking for even a split second that I was going to step aside, and let my group down, made me feel instantly ashamed. I know it sounds corny, but I jumped that night not for me, but for a group of American soldiers I hardly knew at all. I belonged to that team, and by gosh, I was going out that door with my team, for my country!"

And out he went, into the night, landing a minute later like a sack of potatoes onto a grassy plain he couldn't see, with the other members of his team. The next day—in the light of day—they would complete their fifth and final jump and graduate with the pinning on of Airborne wings.

Perhaps Keen is waxing poetic, or, in fact, maybe his sense of belonging to a team had such a strong impact on him that he felt

Team efforts always go better when everyone feels acknowledged.

compelled to jump out of an airplane in complete darkness. However, his claim of team influence seems genuine. Throughout generations of stories about combat, veterans invariably assert that, when the mission was at its toughest and most challenging, the notion of *country* became more a matter of fighting for one's team than for a political system or an ideal.

It's no wonder that the Airborne Creed seamlessly combines the terms *team* and *country* in one of its passages:

> I belong to a proud and glorious team—the Airborne, the Army, my Country. I am its chosen pride to fight where others may not go—to serve them well until the final victory.

A productive sense of belonging does not have to be on the dramatic level Keen describes. Leah Gebhardt is the director of a licensing and copyright team in the music industry. She says that team efforts always go better when everyone feels acknowledged as part of the lineup. "When people all consider themselves equal parts of the group, and when they work together and get along as a coherent team, big projects have a way of getting done." Gebhardt suggests that meeting deadlines or last-minute assignments—such as putting together the copyright work on an album earlier than scheduled—are much easier for a team to handle when everybody knows they are in it together. Gebhardt offers an interesting definition of camaraderie. "It's the combination of friendship and protocol," she offers.

The successful leader understands the need for the dedicated individual to experience a sense of membership and camaraderie. Teams often face tough challenges and long-term endeavors. But when a good worker joins like-minded people in a kinship of cause, there's no stronger satisfaction when success is achieved.

FOR CONSIDERATION:

- Is it easier to get something done when you share the goal with others?

- How does your alliance with a team help your dedication to its cause?

- Is it okay to enjoy being part of a group just for the sense of fellowship or belonging?

The West Pointer Knows the Value of Synergy Among Citizens

Just when West Point plebes think their year-long rite of passage is over, they are thrust into the summer of their sophomore, or yearling, year—referred to tongue-in-cheek as "the best summer of your life." Living and training at Camp Buckner, a wooded site on West Point property located away from the granite buildings and the parade fields that make up the well-known heart of the Academy, yearlings are trained by a cadre composed of senior cadets, or firsties, and an assortment of Regular Army officers and sergeants. The training includes map reading and orientation, platoon-level tactics, and hands-on weapons instruction. Whereas plebe summer has much to do with learning how to be a cadet, yearling summer introduces the class to the more important, practical information on becoming an officer.

The living conditions at Camp Buckner are, to a large extent, miserable. The wooded retreat is isolated, uninspiring, and humid. The barracks are of a World War II vintage. The mosquitoes are plentiful, and they're large enough to carry away small animals (okay, not really). The training has its good moments, but the "hurry up and wait" logistics of getting large numbers of people to various training locations is numbing. Most cadets are much more interested in the training they'll do with real Army units during their junior and senior summers. Camp Buckner is an uninspired simulation of the Army, where everyone carries the same repeating thought: "I'd much rather be somewhere else."

To its credit, the Buckner experience teaches an urgent lesson, perhaps *the* urgent lesson: everyone brings something different to the table. That is, everyone has a talent that can be used during squad training, and, when combined, these talents blend in a complementary way to get the job done. For example, every squad has that person with a natural sense of direction, and putting that person at "point" to lead the team keeps that squad from spending the night lost in a remote location when the sunlight runs out. Every squad has a well-spoken lecturer, able to brief the site officer or evaluator on how the squad plans to approach a particular mission. (Getting a GO at any particular site has as much to do with confident presentation as it does with execution.) Every squad has a fusspot, who ensures everybody leaves the garrison area with the appropriate gear in their rucksacks (backpacks) and an adequate supply of water. Every squad has a rumor miner, who keeps them posted on the latest behind-the-scenes talk about upcoming training and possible leave time (time off) for good performance. Very often, these personalities are radically different and not necessary harmonious, or even sociable. But if the squad leader manages them and holds them together, their individual talents tend to mesh in such a way that the squad goes on to perform well and accomplish necessary tasks.

Perhaps the best demonstration of this synergy is an unusual obstacle course at Camp Buckner that yearlings have to complete as squads. Either the entire squad finishes each obstacle or the entire squad fails, regardless of how well an individual cadet might be doing. A typical obstacle involves several stationary posts in the ground of various heights and distances, and a number of two-by-four boards of different lengths. In order to negotiate across the posts, the boards must be placed in such a manner that, once everyone is across one or two posts, they can be reconfigured and reused in a different way toward the next set of posts. Strategizing is important, as there's no turning back for anything left behind, and sometimes leaving boards behind is necessary to advance forward. Furthermore, squads need to consider who goes first and who can help others across obstacles, as sometimes strength is most contributing, and sometimes being small allows the leader to wiggle across and through an obstacle and position a board for the larger members to go across. What clearly comes out of such an exercise is that the combined calling out and cooperating of ideas and the pooled attributes of the squad members transports the entire squad from Point A to Point B. Even the smartest and most athletic squad member could not negotiate the obstacles alone.

A cadet learns that such is the way with a community or a country where people thrive by offering a variety of goods and services to each other for the personal benefit of commerce and the communal benefit of mutual societal enhancement.

I remember carrying this lesson with me into my life after the Army. As a manufacturing and logistics manager, I often was placed in charge of teams with a variety of talents and competencies and, for that matter, work preferences. Sometimes it made sense to have one person repair and repackage damaged material and another person load the trucks if that's what each of them preferred to do and was better at doing, rather than having everyone repair and repackage and then having everyone load the trucks. Other times, mixing it up a bit was good for cross-training and reassessing of skills. But one thing remained constant: the collection of talents and specialties was always better than simply multiplying the talent and specialty of one worker.

The team that builds on the individual strengths of its members eventually becomes a whole that's much greater than the sum of its parts.

Sure, an organization could get by with everybody tending to themselves. But just like the barber giving haircuts to the dentist who fills his cavities, the team that builds on the individual strengths of its members eventually becomes a *whole* that's much greater than the sum of its parts.

FOR CONSIDERATION:

- Do you have a unique talent that can—and perhaps already does—benefit your team?

- Can you name one positive thing that each member of your team does to support the mission?

- How do the diverse talents of many people blend together to benefit the entire group?

- Why do the collective achievements of a ten-person group often exceed the combined achievements of ten individuals?

The West Pointer Desires Harmony Among Soldiers

Here's an interesting way to celebrate diversity: push uniformity!

When West Point appointees show up at the Academy on Reception Day, they bring a variety of skills and talents. Some of them are great athletes, sought out for the skills they bring to the Army's representation in collegiate sports. Others are near-geniuses, attracted to West Point's academic programs, including majors in computer science and nuclear engineering. Others are gifted sons and daughters of successful military people, hoping to follow the paths of their parents. Others are Army soldiers who have shown the potential to be good officers. (About one in six appointees to West Point is an enlisted soldier in the Regular Army, Army Reserve, or National Guard.) A handful of arrivals are talented foreign students, sent to the Academy by allies of the United States. And, finally, some of these new cadets are simply well-qualified, energetic young people from all walks of life throughout America.

They come from all different backgrounds. Some of them arrive with their parents in fancy cars, dressed for success. Others show up in beat-up family vehicles, barely able to make it over Bear Mountain. And others arrive by themselves via transportation from Newark Liberty Airport with old, tattered luggage, unaccompanied because their parents couldn't afford the trip or the time away from work. Some have spent their last dollar on the ride to West Point.

These new appointees are from different religions, races, and ethnicities. They bring different hope and goals. They are as assorted as a Mother's Day box of candy.

But that doesn't last long.

As mentioned earlier, a lot happens on R-Day. The men have their hair cut; the women have theirs tied back. They are all fitted for their white-over-gray warm weather uniforms. The uniforms are tailored on the spot, and these new cadets put them on, packing away their civilian clothing for the summer. They are issued black shoes, white caps, and white gloves.

They are assigned to their training companies. Throughout the afternoon, they are given a crash course on how to march in formation to the beat of a bass drum.

Incredibly, this transformation comes together in one day. During late afternoon, at the main parade field on the Plain, the bleachers are filled with those parents and friends who could make the trip. As the marching band plays the West Point March, these new cadets—about thirteen hundred of them—march out in uniform, following their senior cadet trainers. Raising their right hands, they are sworn in as new cadets, thus accepting their appointments and beginning their tough journey. And then they march back into the cadet barracks, leaving thousands of onlookers both saddened that they couldn't say good-bye one more time and flat-out stunned by the change that only one day has brought.

> *That's what successful management is all about: tapping into individual strengths while keeping everyone focused on a common goal.*

This one-day whirlwind of activity isn't meant just as a drill to impress a crowd of proud parents. It is meant to convey the message to these young people, as quickly and as compellingly as possible, that they are now "identical." They have the same clothing and the same purpose. More importantly, they are about to be addressed the same way by their trainers, meaning their fine clothing or book smarts or athletic ability no longer makes them stand out as they might have in high school. They are of equal standing.

Paradoxically, over the summer and throughout plebe year, these new members of the Corps become acutely aware of their differences: uniforms and cut hair might be meant to de-emphasize differentiation, but instead it tends to accentuate it. However, the dissimilarities that might have caused friction and discord among groups in other settings do not have such an effect among new cadets. There's a kind of a harmony among them, brought about by a common thread—a commonality of objective—that that runs through this mesh of people brought together by the oddest of circumstances. By pushing uniformity and underscoring mutual objectives, the Academy ironically instills harmony and celebrates diversity.

And such it could be for any leader. Instead of drawing attention to the differences among team members—differences that otherwise might cause friction—the leader should empha-size some standardization and conformity and sameness of mis-sion. The leader may find that people will tend to seek innovation within the parameters they've been given and to appreciate the unique qualities among themselves that bring about this innovation. The end result is a condition of accept-ance of and appreciation for each other's differences.

Fraud prevention manager John Barry suggests another rea-son for instilling at least some standardization: it makes man-agement on a large-scale level easier to handle. "When I travel to different fraud units throughout the country," he says, "it is gratifying when I leave one location, show up at another, and the visits strike me as seamless. It means the right things are happening in different places." Barry concurs with the idea that setting rules encourages, rather than discourages, innova-tion. "If you give a team a set of guidelines to work within, it will find creative ways to improve performance while follow-ing the rules."

The West Pointer understands that devotion to cause means sharing the cause. The winning leader puts an accent on the team's common purpose and pushes for conformity, which in turn celebrates diversity and the differences among team members.

And that's what successful management is all about: tapping into individual strengths while keeping everyone focused on a common goal.

FOR CONSIDERATION:

- Why is it necessary to emphasize the common goals of the team?

- In what good ways does conformity de-emphasize differences? In what good ways does it paradoxically draw attention to them?

- Why do differences among people sometimes cause friction and hostility?

- Can harmony exist among team members with differences?

The West Pointer Is Dedicated to the Greater Idea

During their four years at West Point, cadets go through four distinctive and predictable phases. Plebe year entails the shock of being a plebe, and yearling year entails the shock of *no longer* being a plebe! Cow year, when cadets assume roles compatible with those of noncommissioned officers in the Army, usually consists of taking the role of leader seriously—perhaps too seriously. The third-year cadet feels a deep obligation to take charge of the squad, maintain an atmosphere of discipline, and complete an overwhelming set of tasks and responsibilities. Firstie year, strangely enough, involves the transformation into what initially seems like a less-concerned manner. The firstie, at some point, appears to younger cadets to be more preoccupied with graduation and all it holds than with the mundane activities of the Corps. The assessment of these younger cadets is understandable, but erroneous.

In my cow year, I remember feeling beleaguered by the duties of maintaining a squad plus taking care of my own academic and cadet-related obligations. Carl Fossa, a firstie in my cadet company, noted my distress. "Problems?" he asked.

"Yeah," I said, "I've reached a point where I'm pretty sure everything's going to fall apart." Since he seemed in the listening mood, I offered in detail how several duties were about to clash with some academic requirements. "It really seems like the end is never in sight, doesn't it?"

Fossa offered a different take on my problem. "You've been here for almost three years, and I think you still don't get the idea."

"Which is—?"

"You're supposed to fail. The end is *never* in sight, the job is *never* done, and for the rest of your time in the Army, no job will *ever* really get done. What you have to do is concentrate on the process, not the completion, and try to do some good along the way. That's the idea." And with that thought, he left the room.

Concentrate on the process rather than the completion, and do some good along the way. At that point, I think I began to understand why so many firsties were the way they were: instead of getting bogged down with the daily hodgepodge of silly cadet tasks and requirements, they dedicated themselves to the greater idea being represented. It was not indifference: it was keeping things in perspective.

And for the West Pointer who finally understands that belief, there is much inner peace and a feeling of purpose. The West Pointer lives by the notion that there is a greater good and a greater reason that transcends the person and the team. Dedication to such an ideal is what ultimately bonds the team and keeps its members laser-focused.

It's easy to see why the Academy is filled with symbols of these greater reasons. The statues of great patriots populate the Plain just outside the barracks where most cadets live. Large chapels for three different religious denominations are within walking distance. And the oldest cadet barracks on post, at the center of everything, houses the assembly room where Honor Code hearings are held. Whether it is based on patriotism or spirituality or morality, accepting and taking on a greater rationale for doing things gives the leader a feeling of purpose and a reason for pushing on with the team.

Trudging through a mishmash of problems—not to mention the daily task of "putting out fires"—becomes a lot easier when seen as contributing to this larger vision.

Just as importantly, embracing the concept of a grand scheme allows leaders to ask tough things of their teams. Handing out assignments one by one in the order they're created quickly becomes tedious, and with each new task, the means for getting them accomplished (positive reinforcement, negative reinforcement, pleading, etc.) seems less like leadership and more like nagging. But once the grand scheme or the greater good is introduced, the leader presents the purpose and the vision with each new task. Projects can now be grouped according to where they fit into the design, and people can walk away with assignments understanding their urgency and their ultimate benefit. Finishing a task becomes akin to adding another piece to the puzzle, and ordinary jobs become small but critical contributions to the mission. Each team member feels important and useful.

It also is important that the pieces of the puzzle stay interlocked. Aircraft engine design engineer Chuck Granitz says that no single department can isolate itself and still consider itself part of the big picture. "For example, people

> *Successful leaders devote themselves to a bold ideal and channel their teams to fulfilling it.*

from different design groups have to be fully aware of how their designs will impact each of the other systems on the engine. Turbines have to be interested in what's going on with the aero, combustor, and compressor folks, as does the frame, bearings, and controls people, and how it all relates to making better engines. People can't detach themselves if they want to stay focused on a grand design." Successful leaders devote themselves to a bold ideal and channel their teams to fulfilling it.

FOR CONSIDERATION:

- Why is it valuable to understand and dedicate oneself to a greater idea or philosophy?

- Is there something calming and gratifying about believing in a greater cause for all our energy and efforts?

- How might devotion to a greater cause help you lead your team?

The West Pointer Allows the Freedom to Criticize

Marshall Carter, West Point Class of 1962, is perhaps *the* distinctive example of taking the useful tenets of combat leadership and applying them to business.

Upon graduation from the Academy, before he made his laudable mark in the world of finance, Carter broke free from a family lineage of high-ranking Army officers and instead chose the Marine Corps as his branch of service. He served fourteen years as a Marine Corps officer, including two tours in Vietnam: first as a rifle company commander in the mid-1960s, then as an advisor to the Vietnamese Marines in the early 1970s. His military awards included the Navy Cross, the Bronze Star, and the Purple Heart.

His foray into the business sector reached a pinnacle with his position as chairman and CEO of the financial services giant, State Street Bank and Trust Company, from 1992 to 2001. Under Carter's leadership, State Street's assets under management grew from $66 billion to $720 billion, and its business base expanded from thirty-two to ninety countries. He currently teaches leadership and business at Harvard's Center for Business and Government and at MIT's Sloan Business School.

Listening to Marshall Carter's plainspoken thoughts about today's business world, one perceives a feeling of dismay that more managers aren't embracing the principles of responsibility, integrity, and dedication. "Managers today are under tremendous pressure from several fronts," he notes. "I get the feeling that many of them haven't been trained to stand firm against this pressure."

Carter believes a leadership problem occurs when knowledgeable people on the team are not given the freedom to pass judgment on their manager's decisions or on the direction the team as a whole is taking. "One of the principles of military leadership that carries over well into all types of management is the idea of encouraging criticism within the organization," he says. That is, a leader should promote candid analysis and feedback rather than have everyone buy into a plan simply because the leader likes it. Carter offers several pointers for the manager who wants genuine, useful feedback from team members.

First, the leader must openly encourage dissent. "A manager should openly compliment the person who comes forward with a differing view," says Carter, "and should make it known that others are expected to do the same." Once people perceive that a thoughtful difference of opinion is not politically incorrect, they will be less likely to sit quietly in a conference room while a bad decision takes on a life of its own. People also should be persuaded to question the information that leads to a decision. A diversity of aptitude and ideas is useless if people believe that unspoken approval is the norm.

> *The proper time to critique a plan is before it has been implemented and not after, unless new and compelling circumstances come along.*

Second, Carter suggests that managers should request feedback in ways that will not allow peer pressure to take over. If someone has a solution that might be unpopular or difficult to carry out, he might be inclined not to bring it up. On the other hand, if a team member feels passionately about a solution, she might garner support for it over water cooler and lunch conversations, working the team before the decision-making meeting comes around. In both cases, the best resolution might be getting buried by the presence of forceful and capitulating personalities. A way to combat such peer pressure is to request ideas via email and then discuss each of them in a conference room without attributing a name to each alternative. A tough but effectual plan might be brought forward and implemented if its creator isn't embarrassed by the initial resistance from peers looking for an easy (but inadequate) solution.

Third, Carter proposes that, if conference rooms are places for silent, peer-induced, or boss-induced consent, then feedback and decision-making should be taken out of them. Replacing meetings with one-on-one management immediately removes the conference room from the equation. "One-on-one management not only brings about better communication," he observes, "but it allows a person to offer the boss suggestions without worrying about what others are thinking." Effective one-on-one management includes creating a rapport with each team member, having them personally support the priorities of the team, setting personal goals, and then following up on each person's progress. It also involves lots of listening. Along the way, each team member becomes at ease with the idea of giving the boss genuine, helpful feedback, even if it runs contrary to the boss's initial take on a topic.

Finally, the leader should consider taking the one-on-one process a step further by seeking good people where they work. "People are always more comfortable in their own settings," says Carter. "If you make it a point to regularly walk around and catch people along the way, people will be much more inclined to tell you what's on their mind." Such *management by walking around* philosophy is nothing new to the art of effective leadership. But Carter makes an especially important observation: when the expected walls of management hierarchy—a manager's aloofness, the distance across a conference room table, the obstruction of a boss's desk—are torn down, people want to help, and such a desire from key employees is crucial.

The key word is *casual*. That's not to suggest that a manager become "one of the gang" or that one should put an end to the professional, respect-driven relationship between a manager and a team member. But if a manager can maintain an aura of authority while addressing people casually, away from the *edifices* of authority, people are likely to offer valuable opinions.

The leader should impress upon the team that there are proper times and places for criticism. For example, the proper time to critique a plan is before it has been implemented and not after, unless new and compelling circumstances come along.

If someone is not an active player in the initial decision-making process, his criticism after the fact sounds petty and detrimental to morale. The proper place includes the conference room and wherever the boss might be addressing the person one-on-one. But when criticism is removed from (i.e., "behind the backs of") the key decision-makers, it can seem small and caustic, rather than supportive and contributing—even if the criticism is valid.

The West Pointer doesn't look for a team of "yes-men." Instead, he permits team members to share concerns, voice objections, and make recommendations—as long as this input is respectful and productive.

FOR CONSIDERATION:

- What is to be gained from encouraging criticism within a team?

- Why do people hesitate to criticize, even if it's condoned and encouraged?

- How could you better make your team members comfortable with offering constructive commentary?

- Is there a proper time to voice objections? Is there an improper time?

The West Pointer Serves as Cheerleader for the Big Picture

Americans over the ages have maintained a fairly consistent quality: we tend to put a face on all successes, failures, and challenges. Popular history regarding the United States' fight for independence, for example, centers more on the people of the time than their actions: a colorful cast of characters such as George Washington and Benjamin Franklin occupy our lore and our imaginations. Our national achievements are often tied closely with the leaders of the era, such as Abraham Lincoln (an end to slavery and secession), Franklin D. Roosevelt (an end to the Great Depression), and John F. Kennedy (setting a bold direction for the U.S. space program). Instead of condemning the atrocities of the world, we put a face on those atrocities and demonize those faces (Hitler, Noriega, Osama bin Laden). In sum, we often deal with issues and crusades in the context of heroes and villains.

The same is true for military and business leadership. We're inclined to concentrate our views of grand campaigns on the personalities who led them, such as Grant, MacArthur, and Schwarzkopf. And we very much like to attribute the strategies and successes of corporations to the CEOs in charge at the time of triumph. Even the most astute financial analysts have a difficult time separating the company from the human icon in charge. Not surprisingly, we also tend to accredit the failure of a military operation or a business venture just as easily to that one face, that one person who embodies the grand strategy or conglomerate.

The peculiar aspect of this personification is that it runs contrary to many of today's management philosophies. Much of the leadership training in universities and in companies de-emphasizes the manager as focal point and, instead, dictates the benefits of team building and collective problem-solving. Decision-by-committee is the prescribed manner for settling on a proposal and, subsequently, meetings mushroom and abound. It's no wonder that, when such a philosophy is tripped up by reality, a sure-footed leader eventually must gather up the pieces, unite the team, and set a new course.

Rather than wasting time with the watered-down, feel-good methods of team gratification, West Pointers are taught early on to simply accept our cultural tendency to identify an organization through its leader. From the moment cadets begin their training, they are taught that teams gravitate toward their leaders and that people on the outside recognize the team through its leadership. The West Pointer has no qualms with becoming the heart of the team, even if it means taking all the criticism for a failed team mission.

> *A conscientious team leader accepts that responsibility and offers positive reinforcement whenever the team pushes a little closer to fulfilling the mission.*

In many ways, the leader *is* the team, serving as its rallying point, as its cheerleader for the big picture. A conscientious team leader accepts that responsibility and offers positive reinforcement whenever the team pushes a little closer to fulfilling the mission—always relating the praise and reward back to the big picture.

FOR CONSIDERATION:

- Is it a good thing or a bad thing that we tend to associate the successes or failures of an organization with the person in charge?

- Is it fair to put all the blame or credit on the person at the helm?

- If you know you're the center of attention as a manager, how can you embrace that role and take advantage of it?

- How can you best personalize the mission of your team and serve as its crusader and champion?

CHAPTER FOUR

MISSION

KNOW THE TASK, LIVE THE TASK, PROMOTE THE TASK

The West Pointer Puts Everyone on the Same Sheet of Music

The orchestrated manner in which ten U.S. soldiers can swing twenty tons of field artillery metal into a firing position has never ceased to impress me. Driving along the only road cutting across that part of the desert, the cannon crew got a radio call to send a few hundred-pound rounds five miles into the air, ten miles across the map, and onto an unsuspecting enemy position that one of our forward observers had just spotted. As the truck left the road for the nearest level spot on the right, I enjoyed watching the Army's version of the Bolshoi Ballet.

The truck hauling the cannon in tow—and carrying the crew, their equipment, and lots of rounds—veers and turns. Pulling alongside a sergeant facing the approximate direction of fire, the truck stops on a dime, with soldiers and shovels pouring out the back. The sergeant in charge of this crew rarely says a word, as each soldier knows exactly what to do.

The sergeant and one soldier run to the left side of the cannon and two other soldiers go to the right side. Separating the two sides of the cannon's frame, called the "trails," the soldiers then attach a spade to each trail. As the gun tube is lowered, two more soldiers level and orient it more directly toward a direction, or azimuth, of fire. The howitzer drops onto a stationary plate as its hydraulic pressure is released. The remaining soldiers improve the gun's point of reference and unload and prepare rounds for firing. If the process takes more than five minutes, the crew will consider it a botched effort. And if rounds aren't sailing "downrange" onto an unsuspecting enemy—with the forward observer reporting on and adjusting the fire—within a minute after that, the mission will be considered a failure.

Any good manager has a hand in worthwhile training.

Often, this routine would contribute to a larger sequence, as seven more cannon crews would take part in the same drill, putting enough steel on the target to ensure that, when we reached the area later in the day, it would be safe for our arrival.

Years later, working as a shift manager for International Paper Company, I would be amazed at the similarity of a cannon crew's drill to the synchronization of a production crew trying to thread a sheet of paper through the different parts of a paper machine. During this procedure, ten workers stage themselves at different parts of the machine and make a mechanical process look magical. A team of four workers mixes together wood fiber, recycled paper, water, and chemicals into a series of giant "stock chests." The beater room engineer sends the blend through a few refiners. The machine tender pulls the blend into the "head box," a pressurized tank, and controls the flow of that mixture over a fast-moving conveyor, sending a thin stream of liquid paper through a series of drains and presses. The back tender and the third hand thread this thin, continuous line of wet paper through several dozen rolling dryer cans. The fourth hand, using an air wand, ensures the strand makes it through the dryer section.

As this continuous line of paper works its way through these different stages, the paper is widened to a few inches, then a few feet, and then across the entire width of the machine. As it expands out to produce a large sheet, a fifth hand checks that it is caught properly onto a reel drum that gathers the paper into giant rolls. If at any point in the process everyone is not perfectly in sync, the fragile paper will break, forcing the crew to start over again. Just as with setting up cannons to fire, time is of the essence, since a paper machine without a sheet of paper running across it costs the company lots of money. And similar to a cannon crew, a paper machine crew will be disappointed if the entire drill takes longer than five minutes.

The similarities between these two scenarios extend into how they are managed. Lots of training is involved, and any good manager has a hand in worthwhile training. But before the practicing ever started, each crew was taken through a "walk-through, talk-through" exercise. Stationed at their equipment, with their lieutenant or shift manager listening, the team members individually talked themselves through each of their tasks. The leader would ask questions and make sure that people understood what was going on with them and around them. These drills weren't taught in a classroom or discussed in a conference room. The "walk-through, talk-through" took place in the same environment that the actual drill would take place, with people at their appropriate places.

Such a method of synchronizing is not limited to weaponry or machinery. As an administrator at Seton Hall University, I watched and learned from a financial aid supervisor as she talked her team through each step of processing and approving federal student loans for nontraditional, distance-learning students. After the drill, anybody on her staff could explain what was expected of them or anyone else around them. No machinery involved—just computers, desks, and being on the same wavelength.

Rich Vincz is a supply and production supervisor with thirty years of experience managing teams from eight to eighty strong. He suggests that cross-training has a lot to do with putting people on the same page. "Cross-training, especially on-the-job cross-training, brings everyone into line. It makes people understand the skills of other team members and how long other tasks take." He also notes that it helps everyone to appreciate the contribution others are making.

The hands-on leader understands the benefit of having everyone in step with the plan. Talking people through their responsibilities at their own work stations is an effective way to keep the team humming in unison.

FOR CONSIDERATION:

- What are the advantages to having a team function in harmony and in synchronization?

- Are there examples in your organization where people need to function together or in a specific order?

- Are there examples in your organization where time is of the essence?

- Why not simply conduct a "walk-through, talk-through" in a conference room? Why do people need to be at their work stations?

The West Pointer Supervises Task Preparation

Colonel George W. Goethals knew a thing or two about preparing for a task and seeing it through. A West Point graduate and Army engineer at the turn of the twentieth century, he was asked to take over the languishing construction of the Panama Canal, the grand waterway of access water portals, locks, and dams connecting the Atlantic Ocean with the Pacific Ocean in Central America. The colossal project—which already had included twenty years of digging—was at a standstill. The French company that had built the Suez Canal and was enmeshed in the Panama plan had become financially ruined when it became evident that a sea-level canal would have to be scrapped in favor of chambers, or locks. Disease, mudslides, and machine insufficiency also had contributed to their predicament. Although the rough plans for a canal through Panama had been drawn up four hundred years earlier, the vision still had not been realized.

Goethals took on his position as chief engineer three years after the United States decided to assume control of the project. He did not approach the job lightly. Surrounding himself with a trusted staff—he had gone to school with a few of them—he planned the task in such a way that his team would not suffer the same fate previously endured by others.

Goethals helped design the lock plan that would prove triumphant. He put together a series of steps to improve the working conditions along the Zone. He ensured that the proper amount of dynamite was ordered. He selected an appropriate size and number of steam shovels that could overpower and work past the clay and mud sliding. He planned for the hiring of local workers that eventually would grow to forty thousand strong. And he stayed around to see the strategy through.

Goethals remained on hand throughout the canal's seven-year construction and continued there as governor of the Canal Zone for an additional two years. Today, the fifty-mile long Panama Canal still provides passage between oceans for thousands of ships, saving the ten-thousand-mile trip around South America. A few years later, Goethals would accomplish another monumental achievement by rescuing the Army's logistics systems during World War I.

The story of this quartermaster extraordinaire is one of leadership and, just as significantly, one of preparation. Goethals is not only highly regarded for how he supervised the task: he is respected for how he supervised the *task preparation*. Consider how you might prepare for an undertaking using the Goethals approach.

Put together a good staff. Don't be shy about asking people you know and trust to help you with a task. Typically, they should be technically competent, and they should have performed well for you in the past. Furthermore, they should be up for another challenge. They should exhibit loyalty, a good nature, and humor when appropriate. When those clay slides in Panama persisted for the American team, if they weren't laughing as they pushed on, then they were crying.

Be technically ready for the job at hand. It is worth mentioning that the person who led the failed Canal project prior to the arrival of the American team was not an engineer. Perhaps there are large building projects that non-engineers can handle, but falling back on the West Point principle of being technically and tactically proficient, one wonders how someone without any practical or intellectual experience might possibly complete any intricate assignment. One thing's for sure: if you're not technically ready, you had better surround yourself with people who are. Goethals was ready for the job. He had a hand in helping to draft the blueprints and ultimately approved the final plan and dimensions for the Canal.

Study the mistakes and successes of the people before you. It would have been folly for Goethals to ignore the history of project managers before him. Examining the failed plans of others ensured he would not repeat those mistakes. Studying the scrapped drawings of a sea-level canal helped him to reinforce his reasoning for the lock plan. On the other side of the coin, building on the successes of past teams made sense, too. For example, by all accounts, the earlier team had chosen the proper tract of land, and had been successful in removing millions of square feet of rock and soil. Tapping into those accomplishments was preferable to, say, choosing a different route and starting the digging from scratch.

Understand the scope of the task. The fact that Goethals took seven years to complete the canal but still finished it ahead of schedule suggests that he understood the size of the monster he was taking on. There's something to be said for comprehending scope and being comfortable with it, even if it extends years into the future. This point is especially vital in an age when people's attention spans are becoming shorter or nonexistent. Know what you are getting into, not only from a cerebral standpoint, but from the aspects of time, space, energy, labor, and other resources.

Don't go forward unless your logistics are in order. Once you know the extent of the task, have plans in place for supplies, transportation, human resources, etc., before you get started. In any one of these areas, assume that planning as you go along will mean trouble. The unsuccessful team began digging before they even knew what they were excavating for. By the time they realized that their design wasn't feasible, their machinery wasn't adequate, and their workforce wasn't healthy, it was too late.

Ensure the size of your team matches the size of the task. Goethals was flexible about the range of his workforce and not afraid to grow his labor into the epic task. Had he set arbitrary hiring limits, the project would have slowed. On the opposite end, over-hiring from the start would have been unnecessarily costly. Constantly reevaluating and matching the head count to the task kept the project dynamic and, again, ahead of schedule. Always be vigilant with the number of heads. People are your most important asset, but in appropriate correlation, they are also your biggest expense.

Stick around. One can easily imagine a project engineer setting the wheels in motion in Central America and then taking off for Florida golf courses as soon as leaving is politically acceptable. Granted, Goethals didn't have access to airplanes, or for that matter, even a car. But taking into account that he stayed on as governor of the Canal Zone until (his first) retirement, the principle of staying on hand to watch the wheels in motion seemed to suit him. Hands-on leaders don't just keep a project going by monitoring progress firsthand; they cultivate achievement by serving as the rallying point for all present.

> *Hands-on leaders don't just keep a project going by monitoring progress firsthand; they cultivate achievement by serving as the rallying point for all present.*

The good leader supervises task preparation with enough technical expertise and deliberation that the groundwork is laid for a plan that will work.

FOR CONSIDERATION:

- When was the last time you jumped into a project that you weren't prepared to take on?

- Why is it important to trust the abilities and the loyalty of your staff?

- How important is technical know-how for the team leader?

- What are some of the ways you might find out about the successes or failures of the team leaders before you?

- Why are logistics often taken for granted?

- What are the benefits to being present when the plan is in progress?

West Pointers Are Unique Because They Follow-Up

Sometimes, there are those days when the stars, the planets, and the moon align in just the right way so that your day goes splendidly. And then there are those days when the gravitational pull of all these heavenly bodies combine to pull a mountain of fertilizer into your direction. I think my entire plebe year was the latter. Back in the 1980s, plebes had to *ping,* meaning they had to walk swiftly, in a silly fashion, looking straight ahead and hugging the walls and stairways when indoors, as if standing at attention while riding a Segway. Today, the practice of making plebes ping is officially prohibited. But at the time of my plebe existence, it was a yearlong way of life. Pinging could be terrifying if you didn't know exactly where you were headed: since you couldn't turn your head to reference room numbers or hallways, if you got lost, the best you could hope for was to be ignored long enough to clear the area and reorient yourself.

One evening, early on in the year, I was attempting to team up with another classmate to work on an academic project. Unfortunately, his room was on the other side of the cadet housing area, in barracks I was completely unfamiliar with. After bouncing off the same walls a few dozen times, I was looking not only exceptionally lost but also terribly disheveled. A third-year cadet, or cow, saw that I was adrift and untidy and smelled my fear from a good distance. "Mis-TAH, get over here," he called.

As a rule, plebes were not supposed to be quizzed on Academy lore after dinner, with the idea that everyone should instead be working on their schoolwork. But, like I said, the planets were working against me. We stood almost nose to nose. After grilling me for about ten minutes—just enough time to keep himself out of trouble—he offered his appraisal.

"You're lost, you're a mess, and you don't know even the most basic plebe knowledge. Mister, you're a disaster."

Curiously, he didn't look at my nametag or ask who I was or take down my name. Instead, he posed a question: "Do you have what it takes?"

"Yes, sir."

"Do you *have* what it takes?"

"YES, SIR!"

A pause. Then: "I want to see you in this same spot, at this same time, exactly one hundred nights from tonight. You'd better look squared away, and you'd better be ready to answer some questions. Understand?"

"Yes, sir."

And he turned and walked away. I went on my way again and, after a few more dead-end turns, I found my academic buddy, and we churned out our report. Later that night, finding my way back to my own room proved substantially easier.

Keep in mind that such grilling sessions between upperclass cadets and plebes happened relentlessly. Chances were that that cow had smoked at least several dozen plebes that day. Considering that my class started with over fourteen hundred plebes, the idea that he might remember me or our appointment one hundred days later was understandably preposterous. And the added fact that he hadn't caught my name might have made the rendezvous justifiably forgettable.

But I didn't forget.

Upon returning to my room that night, I counted out one hundred days, wrote the time and place for that upcoming meeting, and then went on to a million other tasks that were on my mind.

Ninety-nine days later, I saw the scheduled reunion on the calendar. I gave my shoes an extra-good shine that night and studied my handbook of Academy lore, called *Bugle Notes*.

The next night, I made my way over to that building. (Over three months later, I had become familiar with most of the buildings in the cadet area and with how to better navigate while pinging.)

You can guess the rest of the story. He was there. He inspected my uniform, asked me a few questions,

The effective leader takes the important step of following through.

and sent me on my way. The reality of the fact that both of us had made good on the appointment did not surprise or impress us. I never would have gotten in trouble had I ignored or forgotten about his hundred-day-old directive. I didn't expect a reward for showing up, either. But the follow-up, quite plainly, was expected.

While many of these ridiculous rituals have grown obsolete and banned over the years, undoubtedly another cadet is making good on a several-month-old pledge this very minute. It might have something to do with the Honor Code, and keeping one's word, or making good on an expectation. But more likely cadets, early on, internalize the importance of following up. And doing so forever sets them apart.

Many managers set policy or make a demand and then forget about it. The corporate world is filled with wonderful ideas, but little to no implementation. How many of your past bosses, for example, would have returned for that one-on-one meeting a hundred days later? Their tendency not to show up for such an appointment carries over to their likelihood of following through when giving basic directions.

The effective leader takes the important step of following through. By purchasing a calendar or electronic planner, scheduling a productive day of multitasking, and being patient throughout the long-term (100-day?) plan, the leader who follows up on directions and questions becomes distinctive and exceptionally dependable.

You don't have to wait one hundred days to follow up. If you ask team members for information, tell them that you'll follow up two days later. Jot the appointment down in your planner. Two days later ask them where the requested information is. If they don't have it, voice your displeasure, give them one more day, and ensure they see you writing the new appointment in your planner. Unless you're working in a hostile environment (meriting additional measures), they'll have the info for you the second time around. And at the next request, they'll have it for you the first time around.

Music industry licensing and copyright director Leah Gebhardt suggests that managers with the best reputations are the ones known for following up. "The music publishers we deal with have figured out who they can pay little attention to and who will be calling again to check up on requested paperwork. Many times, they react promptly in order to avoid that second or third call." Gebhardt says that another advantage to following up is that managers learn who is dependable and who needs more or less direction. "If you didn't follow up with people, there would be no way to measure how trustworthy they are."

A final thought on following up: it works both ways. That is, if you promise people on your team that you'll research a problem and get back to them the next day, schedule it into your planner and follow through on your promise.

The effective leader is respected for possessing the unusual trait of following through.

FOR CONSIDERATION:

- How skeptical would you be if someone promised you something in exactly one hundred days?

- Why is the tendency to follow up such a unique attribute among team leaders?

- Do you keep your day scheduled in a planner? If yes, does it help you to follow up?

The West Pointer's Team Owns the Mission

Patrick Hynds is the chief technology officer for CriticalSites, Inc., a software development and network operating systems company in New York and New England. He says that the most important thing he learned at West Point about team dynamics didn't become evident to him until years after he had graduated from the Academy and finished his service in the Army.

Hynds's cadet experience and officer experience had shown him the difference that even a small team could make. "If a small team within the bigger organization holds rigid standards and a fanatical determination for perfection, they'll become the center of everything going on in that organization." What Hynds didn't understand was *why* this small team could make such a difference.

Upon leaving the Army, Hynds did not immediately join CriticalSites. Instead, he worked for several companies where he was taken by surprise by the *lack* of such small, industrious teams. He wound up in several corporate environments where, he claims, "people said *yes* but meant *no* and did *no*." He was taken aback by this attitude because he had assumed that well-managed team dynamics always meant a completed task. Furthermore, he had taken for granted that professional people lived up to their promises and their positions within a company. Instead, he discovered that corporate culture often translated into a feeling of separateness—a perception of vast distances between the people and the mission. "What I found," he says, "was a culture where people tended to hide from the objective and skate by."

Being the proactive manager that he was, Hynds neither accepted this attitude nor surrendered to it. He experimented with several methods for bringing enthusiasm, dedication to standards, and a desire for excellence to the teams he led, including breaking down a larger group into smaller, autonomous, and more competitive groups. "I learned to fight the mantra of *blend in and take cover within the larger group*," he says. "I wanted people to step forward with their input and concerns."

By the time Hynds arrived at his current company, he was starting to get a grip on what made some small teams very pivotal within the business. "It had to do with ownership, with personal commitment," he says. "You can exercise all the management techniques you've learned throughout your life, and you can exert all the influence you can on a team, but if they don't feel like they own part of the mission and have a stake in the outcome, they'll never be relevant."

Hynds feels, all these years later, that he has rediscovered the team values he appreciated as a cadet. "I belong to a team that has recaptured the spirit I had missed so much from Academy," he offers. He speaks of managers at the highest levels of his company instilling passion and making everybody feel as if they each possess a small piece of the big solution. "Every small team within our company owns the mission," he says.

Such is the way with West Point training—or, for that matter, any effectual management education. Years later, alumni smack their heads and say, "Ah, so *that's* what they meant!" Cadets themselves do not immediately understand or welcome the notion of full commitment to task. In fact, many cadets initially follow the "2.0 and go" mentality, figuring that the easiest way to make it through the various, crushing requirements at the Academy is to put in the minimum amount of effort necessary to push past each one. But at some point during their four-year stay, West Pointers each have a personal epiphany that causes them to immerse themselves in some aspect of cadet life, often involving an established group or team. And it is the team *ownership* of purpose that instills this newfound captivation and enthusiasm.

The leader's unending charge is to keep igniting sparks of enthusiasm within a team, to keep people committed and loyal, and not just marking time. It hurts walking past a cubicle with a sign that reads "113 months until retirement." But asking the person to pull it down is just asking for resentment. The idea is to make the person feel like such a strong, important participant that he'll *want* to pull it down. The way to do that is to liberally hand out responsibility, to listen intently to the team's feedback and recommendations, and to integrate the team's efforts as much as possible into the organization's grand design.

Lisa Tawney Scheuerman runs her own telemarketing and direct mail marketing company in Maryland. She agrees that small teams owning their missions are what make a larger organization move forward. "It's all about getting people to buy into the team mentally," she says. She notes that, at her business, selling the team and the mission—so to speak—to team members entails giving people responsibilities outside the scope of their regular jobs, and openly acknowledging and rewarding commendable performance. "It

> *The leader's unending charge is to keep igniting sparks of enthusiasm within a team, to keep people committed and loyal, and not just marking time.*

could be something as easy and tangible as pizza or extended breaks," she notes, "or it could be something more deeply motivating such as quarterly sales awards and dinner out for long-term success." Scheuerman observes that ownership usually leads to innovation.

"If members of a particular sales group take on their objective wholeheartedly," she offers, "they'll come up with all kinds of creative ways to achieve it."

She's right. The fundamental power of a small, committed team is the energy that separates the dinosaur marking time until extinction and the ever-evolving organism that's looking to dominate the future.

The good leader keeps the team small, hands out the assignment, sets the rules, and lets the group own the mission with their innovations and team drive.

FOR CONSIDERATION:

- What might prompt a person within an organization to "hide" and wait out the next thirty years?

- Have you seen teams that complete their tasks without ever realizing their potential? What might be the reason?

- What happens to a team once they adopt the mission and commit themselves to it?

- What might it mean for your team to "own the mission"?

The West Pointer Breaks the Task Down
for Everyone to Understand

It's a pity that the term "poop" doesn't get used at West Point as much as it used to. Back when I was a cadet in the mid-1980s, plebes were forever being asked, "What's the poop?" When asked for the "poop," a plebe would snap to attention and provide the three most important stories from that morning's *New York Times*. "Sir, today in the *New York Times*, it was reported that—" And three headlines would follow. If the upperclass cadet wanted additional information about a story or two, it was expected of the plebe to have studied the articles and to be well informed on the subjects.

The phrase "What's the poop?" isn't heard within the Corps like it used to be, but the philosophy lives on. Today's plebes are still expected to know their current events, and when an officer or cadet commander at the Academy asks for the poop, people still understand it means "cut to the chase."

As with Patrick Hynds's story, the best-learned lessons from West Point aren't always apparent at the time. And such is the case with offering the "poop." I remember envying the classmate who could rattle off the happenings of the day from the front page of the paper quickly and clearly without any inconsequential information attached. On the other hand, I had a tendency to ramble, with lots of unimportant fluff hanging onto each story. It was this trivial stuff that led to trivial questions, taking me further and further into the hole I was digging for myself. The lesson at the time was *Stop talking as quickly as possible and you won't talk yourself into difficulty*. But there was a more urgent message that didn't register with me until my time in the Army as an officer.

The message: people are busy, very busy. Yes, given the time, they would love to dive into a topic and learn all they can. But if someone else—particularly someone competent—has already done the research, the group really only has time for the main points and an educated recommendation. As an officer, I quickly broke the habit of including fluff with any briefing, even if the fluff might have added appropriately to the bullet points or might have made known my authority on the topic. Giving only the "poop" became the way of doing business. It's worth noting that, even as a second lieutenant—the plebe of Army officers, if you will—I was expected to know my topic. If asked for an opinion or a recommendation by officers several ranks higher, I accepted the possibility that perhaps, at that very specific point in time, I might have known more about that topic than anyone else in the room. And I offered my opinion accordingly.

Teams, as entities, are busy, too, especially the pivotal teams that make up dynamic organizations. As such, effective leaders must treat their busy teams much the same as they treat busy people. They need to break down a task for their teams to understand. They need to keep it short and concentrate on a few key points, and they need to allow time for questions.

Amy Stredler, a West Point graduate, has been in pharmaceutical sales for about ten years. She currently handles psychiatric medication accounts for

> *Effective leaders must treat their busy teams much the same as they treat busy people.*

Sanofi-Synthelabo, Inc., one of the largest pharmaceutical companies in the world. She says that learning how to communicate the "poop" was one of the most insightful things she took away from the Academy. "The time I get with doctors can be very limited," she says. "It is crucial to condense, say, a ten-page medical study into about three minutes."

One would think that the task of considering new medication might be meandering and tedious. Not so. Stredler's reputation among them was established long ago, and they're comfortable listening to her rapid-fire briefings and taking in the data. Notably, the information gets through to her listeners. "You'd be amazed at how favorably people absorb information in 'poop' style," she claims. "I might as well start my presentation by saying, 'Sir, today in the *Journal of the American Medical Association*, it was reported that—!'"

Stredler says that putting forth information in "poop" format leaves critical time available for answering questions. People on a team appropriately personalize what they hear and, if a team is being managed the right way, everyone brings something different and valuable to the table. The sooner this information session can switch from briefing to Q&A, the sooner individuals in the group can garner distinct, applicable data.

By emphasizing the three most important parts of a task, the successful leader makes the mission understandable and presents it as achievable. Assuming the key people in your team are smart and productive, they don't have time for sermons. Break down the task, keep it simple, and send your good people on their way.

FOR CONSIDERATION:

- Do you appreciate a boss who "cuts to the chase" and explains a project in basic terms? Why do we tend to appreciate such straight-talkers?

- Why do key people tend to prefer bullet-point briefings rather than immersing themselves in a topic? What are the advantages of the undiluted update?

- Do you break down tasks in a clear-cut manner that your team can understand?

- Do you allow time for questions?

The West Pointer Values Mentorship

When promoting the task at hand, the effective leader takes the lobbying effort to a very personal level—by mentoring. Mentoring occurs both formally and informally at West Point. On the formal level, the Corps of Cadets is divided into thirty-two or thirty-six cadet companies, depending on how big Congress desires the Corps to be in any given year. Each company is assigned a tactical officer (TAC), a full-time Army officer whose job it is to point the cadet leadership in the right direction, to ensure the leadership training system is respected and maintained, and to provide guidance to all cadets within the company whenever it is called for. The presence of tactical officers at the Academy is the formal arrangement for providing mentorship to the Corps. (Cadets might add that tactical officers are also good for conducting room inspections, handing out demerits, and dispensing punishments whenever the mood suits.) These cadet companies are divided four ways into regiments, and each regiment has a tactical officer, a lieutenant colonel. Among a cadet's many goals is to never get noticed by or summoned by the regimental TAC. To do so means a much different type of mentoring!

Just as influential to a cadet's development, if not more so, are the informal mentor-disciple relationships that form at West Point. One such bond is the rapport that develops between a cadet and a senior officer outside the realm of the tactical leadership. An example would be a history professor who takes an interest in a cadet and offers advice regarding the Corps and the Army along the way. It is not uncommon for this officer to keep track of this student following graduation. Upon completing a teaching tour at the Academy, if the professor continues an upward progression in the Army, it is possible the two of them might meet again. As a cadet, I was something of a rock as a swimmer—an "intermediate rock" is what I believe they called me. A few years later, I saw one of my swimming instructors again—as a lieutenant colonel and the commander of the battalion where I served as a brand-new lieutenant.

The other type of informal mentoring at West Point exists on the cadet-to-cadet level. Upperclass cadets aren't automatically paired with plebes—no one reaches into a hat to randomly pick their "grasshopper" for the next year. But the best nuggets of advice and the most reassuring words clearly are those offered between cadets of different ranks. For all the personal development and achievement a cadet struggles to realize, no accomplishment is more rewarding than steering a younger cadet through academic or anxiety-related hardship and seeing that cadet make it into the summer. There's more than a passing chance that the mentor will keep track of this younger comrade until Graduation Day, and perhaps into the Army.

The peculiar nature of mentoring is that, for all of its considerable worth, there's really not much to it. The best books or programs on mentoring easily can be reduced to a three-by-five card. A person within an organization takes on a junior member of the group as something of a friend and disciple, serving as a company trainer, a listening post, and a career advisor. The arrangement is beneficial for a mentor who can point good people in a direction that's rewarding for them and the team. The setup also is beneficial for the disciples who can learn from experience and go about their business knowing that someone higher up in the organization is on their side.

If making people productive means first getting them to feel important, then mentoring is the ultimate method for doing that. As mentioned before, people contribute most constructively to a team when they feel they are an essential part of it and when they believe they own a stake in its direction and success. Having the attention of a senior person on the team—even in tutoring mode—gives the team member a sense of worth and a feeling that perhaps there's a long-term investment of time and effort taking place. Everyone at least intuitively understands the value of a senior person's time. That this senior person is spending part of that time with a new team member fosters an awareness of worth, of future contribution.

Oddly, new people within a company rarely rush to find themselves a mentor, formally or informally. Maybe it's because of the preconceptions they hold. Admittedly, when the word *mentor* is uttered, certain unfair images are conjured up, such as that of the old, dusty senior manager who constantly spews nuggets of age-old advice. That's unfair, because the most willing mentors are often the most dynamic managers.

> *In the end, mentoring is good for the team, good for the mentor, and good for business.*

Sure, they might occasionally wax poetic about the old days, but more often, they prefer to listen, allowing the pupil to discover the answers.

Mentoring becomes even more advantageous to the employee when the mentor serves as an advocate for the mentored team or employee. When I was an enlisted soldier at Fort Hood, Texas, an officer who worked in the headquarters of the First Cavalry Division—Major Mike Jones—caught wind of my desire to attend West Point. He almost immediately took me under his wing and briefed me on the requirements for submitting an application. A review of my grades from high school suggested I would do better by first attending the Academy's preparatory school at Fort Monmouth, New Jersey, where enlisted soldiers under consideration for appointment to West Point brush up on math and English. I completed my application to the prep school and subsequently was accepted. A year later, I successfully gained admission into the Academy. During my prep school time and my early years at West Point, I made a point of writing to Major Jones, updating him on my progress and looking forward to his responding letters of advice. As it turned out, he must have been very much an expert on the West Point admissions process: at this time—and quite coincidentally—Colonel Mike Jones is the West Point Director of Admissions.

Mentors are influential in that people desperately try to avoid disappointing them. One of my first civilian jobs following my time in the Army was with International Paper Company at its paper mill in Oswego, New York. The mill manager, Chris Mallon, not only hired me for the job of shift manager but made a point of often taking me around the mill and grilling me on the different stages of the papermaking process. I remember how disappointed I would be if I finished a walk-through with more questions unanswered than answered. Trying not to let him down became just as basic as making lots of quality paper on a shift.

Tom Glynn is an electrical and mechanical engineer who serves as the building's operations manager for a major financial services corporation. He remembers taking on the mentor role in training and encouraging a heating, ventilation, and air-conditioning mechanic on his team. "I recognized him from the start as someone I'd be able to count on," says Glynn. "Mentoring him and setting him loose on projects was rewarding for both of us. I remember the main point I made to him. 'If you think I won't like it, then don't do it that way.' Otherwise, I didn't really try to mold him in my fashion—I was more interested in showing him leadership qualities, some technical insight, and then letting him develop his own style." In time, Glynn's mechanic went on to become a chief engineer for the company.

Glynn suggests that mentoring means showing partisans how to do things safely, professionally, and effectively.

Besides influencing the team, mentoring is good for the mentor in other ways. Being in a position to help others first means being on top of one's game. It's difficult to give advice or point people along a gainful career path without taking stock of what's going on in an organization or a professional field. And it's nearly impossible to listen to the problems of underlings without relating to those setbacks in a personal way, perhaps fast-forwarding them to a few years later and seeing oneself. Mentoring others has therapeutic side-effects of self-evaluation and personal career appraisal.

In the end, mentoring is good for the team, good for the mentor, and good for business. From the first time West Pointers approach a tactical officer, a professor, or another cadet for help, they discover and learn to cherish the concept of mentoring.

FOR CONSIDERATION:

- Does your organization have a formal arrangement for pairing mentors with new members?

- How does mentoring benefit the disciple? How does it benefit the mentor?

- Why might mentoring make a team member feel more important?

- Who have been the influential mentors in your life?

CHAPTER FIVE

INSIGHT

TREAT YOUR SOLDIERS
AS IF THEY'RE MOST IMPORTANT—
BECAUSE THEY ARE

The West Pointer Knows
the Garbage Collector's Name

I vividly remember taking an essay test as a West Point cadet in Course PL300: Military Leadership. The final exam question was: "Name two maintenance people who work in this building." Several of my classmates—grade conscious as ever—openly and loudly protested the question. "Surely this question doesn't count toward our scores?" they asked.

"Of course it counts," replied the professor, an Army captain. "If you don't know the people immediately surrounding you during your daily routine as a cadet, how well are you going to know your platoon as a lieutenant?" She made a good point—one that has stayed with me over the years. I imagine I'm one of only a handful of administrators in the large institution where I work who says good morning to the maintenance people, calling them by their first names and asking them about their families.

There's something to be said for knowing everyone's name, greeting them, and taking at least a cursory interest in what's on their minds at any particular time. It adds a human touch to management that's very much lacking in our business world, perhaps intentionally so. Many of us have come to believe that it's easier to make the tough decisions, particularly those involving people and policy, if we remain distant and uncaring. We wear our aloofness like padding, protecting us from the lives we're directly or indirectly responsible for. We wrongly believe that it is better to remain indifferent than to address and deal with people as people.

West Pointers recognize the folly of such aloofness. They often display an outward knowledge of their team members and utilize it whenever they greet one of them. As mentioned before, West Pointers remember the concerned firstie who said hello and took time to check up on them, even if they were just lowly plebes.

Knowing something about even the minor players in your organization isn't just an exercise in kindness and compassion; it's good business.

This firstie, by custom, was businesslike and surly, but always interested. West Pointers appreciate the difference, this awareness and consideration for them, and often carry it into their lives as leaders.

Knowing something about even the minor players in your organization isn't just an exercise in kindness and compassion; it's good business. Chances are the smartest businesspeople are the ones who know the names of every person they regularly come in contact with. Why? Because they understand that the support one receives as a manager is like the support a building gets from its structure: it must start at the foundation. A leader can easily be undermined by any team member at any level. Conversely, the backing and reinforcement a leader receives comes from all levels.

A leader essentially has two choices: 1) Announce the tasks and the goals and crack the whip, or 2) Announce the tasks and the goals, show an interest in the team, and enjoy the support that comes naturally from people who know their team leader cares.

Many times I find myself at the receiving end of this splendid management philosophy, especially when starting work in a new organization. I walk past someone who says, "Hello, Scott." I smile and return the greeting, and then I move along briskly, embarrassed that I don't know who the person is. More often than not, when I learn the person's name, I find that he's pretty high up the food chain. "How on earth does he know who I am?" I wonder. And that's when it occurs to me—*I'm* the garbage collector! Well, relatively speaking, that is. I've joined an organization where the leader finds it worthwhile to know everyone's name.

It's nothing short of remarkable how much more important you make people feel by saying "hello." Adding their names to the greeting magnifies the feeling: someone's name, after all, is subconsciously the most important word that person hears throughout the day. In light of all those studies done on organizational management and leadership theory, how is it that something as easy as a common courtesy can be so crucial to good management, and yet so disregarded and unpracticed?

Engineer and building operations manager Tom Glynn agrees. "I know everyone in my building—everyone," he says. "It makes all the difference in the world saying hello to the night janitor and knowing him by name, acknowledging him as a person." Glynn says something as effortless as a name can build morale and foster allegiance. "Hearing your name causes you to feel real," he notes. "And when a supervisor makes you feel that way, you're more likely to keep that manager informed. You're also more inclined to do things the way he asks you to do them."

Remember, at some point you're going to need more from workers than just their talent and clock-time. You're going to need their cooperation, their humor, their thoughtfulness, and their passion. You're going to need them to go above and beyond the call of duty. These are all *human* attributes, having little to do with logistics and policy. In other words, to get the job done, you're inevitably going to need people to act *human*. So why not treat them that way from the start?

FOR CONSIDERATION:

- Who are the "minor players" in your life right now? The sanitation worker, the mail carrier, the delivery person, the part-time staffer, the new hire? Are they really as "minor" as one might think they are?

- Do you know the names of any of these players? Do you say hello?

- Who are the "minor players" on your team? Again, how "minor" are they?

- Have you ever found out something extraordinary and inspiring about a "minor player" in your life or on your team? What was your reaction? Did it change the way you approached that person? Why?

- Has a "minor player" ever presented you with a major idea?

The West Pointer Learns About People First

Team assessment is what West Pointers do best. Whereas the conventional manager chooses to get an assignment underway and to make things happen fast, it is the *leader* who takes strong, quiet, patient steps, lets the mission wait a while, and begins the process by appraising the team. With such a front-loaded investment, the team eventually seizes the moment and achieves all. Rather than jumping directly into the task at hand, the West Pointer takes inventory of team talents, their character strengths, their aspirations, and their mettle.

To the skeptic, the image of a dozen new cadets sitting around a campfire and explaining why they each came to West Point might seem clichéd. But it is an accurate image. I remember my first field exercise during cadet basic training, or Beast Barracks. Our firstie squad leader, Cadet Ed Dollar, made it a priority on several occasions to pull his squad away from the main bivouac area and to get to know its members better. "What part of the country are you from? What are your hobbies? Why are you here? What do you hope to get out of this place?" He listened intently while we elaborated on ourselves. I suppose his carefree manner might have been frowned upon by his colleagues, and it certainly contradicted the other ninety-five percent of the time he spent yelling at us.

The chats put us at ease enough to let our guard down and reveal our human side, and undoubtedly he considered seeing this side essential to his mission of getting us prepared for the four years ahead. I dare say that, by the end of the summer, he knew more about us than we knew about each other. During these campfire conversations, I gathered he also was assessing the general morale and concerns of the squad.

In the end, I don't think any of us found Cadet Dollar any friendlier or more lenient than the bulk of cadet trainers running us through the wringer. And I'm not convinced these get-togethers made him any more approachable. But learning our human side meant understanding a lot more about his team than other squad leaders. And if the human aspect of team members is the foundation and forecaster of performance, then he was in a position to know how well we were going to cope and to make suitable adjustments earlier on in our training.

West Point graduate Marc McCreery served in the U.S. Army as an A-Team leader for the Army's Special Forces (Green Berets). He currently works as a technology manager for General Electric's consumer products division. McCreery learned early on about the value of examining the character attributes of his team members. "You can size up a person in a conversation or two," he says. "By the time the discussion is done, you generally know if you're dealing with a dud or a stud." Of course, strength of character doesn't always coincide with good job performance. But if one is apparently strong-willed and eager to jump into an undertaking, learning and competence often follow. On the other hand, if a team member presents himself on hesitant footing and seems unsure, then the leader needs to recognize that trait, work on it, or, if necessary, work around it.

> *Getting to know your people as people helps you bridge the gap between what's important to the team and what's essential to the organization.*

Getting to know your people *as people* helps you bridge the gap between what's important to the team and what's essential to the organization or the mission. Michael Ramundo, a professional trainer, explains in his book *The Complete Idiot's Guide to Motivating People*: "You need to know what's important to them, and have a sense of how they feel about issues and situations." It's not always possible to tie a mission directly to the interests of the team members. But if you don't know what those interests are, then you'll *never* make the connection for them.

Learning about the interests and opinions of your team also tells you about what makes them tick—and what gets them ticked off! Nothing works against a manager more than not anticipating group hostility or collective disinterest by the team. Understanding the likes, dislikes, and predilections of the team members helps the leader anticipate reactions and plan accordingly. It also helps the leader decide how to present a mission to the team—how to make it more interesting and appealing. Says Michael Ramudo: "You need to be able to anticipate how they'll respond to events and problems. This is important because their reaction to events controls how you should present those events."

When learning about your people, make a point of ignoring the rumors that have preceded them. There may be some truth to them, and there may not. But learning for yourself what a person is all about allows that person a clean slate from which to start and ignores the subjectivities and potential mean-spiritedness of others. Besides, what was truth to someone else might not be truth to you. Suppose someone tells you that your new member, John, is unmotivated. Well, perhaps he was under a different set of circumstances—including a different leader. A new set of conditions might make for a new and improved John. As Marc McCreery puts it, "If they've got a reputation, let them start a new one—a better one."

When assessing your team members, find out about their individual ambitions and aspirations. Where do they want to be in a year? In five years? If they're content to stay put, you need to know that, too. What do they value? A soldier once said to me, "Sir, my goal each month is to go another thirty days without anyone messing with my beer, my girlfriend, or my free time." That statement might have seemed a bit coarse on the surface. But looking deeper, he was merely stating that he valued relaxation, companionship, and time for himself—clear-cut life objectives for any working person.

Getting to know your people and what's on their minds puts you light years ahead of other managers in getting things done.

FOR CONSIDERATION:

- Have you ever jumped into a task without first learning more about your team members? What happened?

- While chatting with a member of your team, what suggested to you that this person had strength of character?

- What are the interests of your team members? Their dislikes? What do they have strong opinions about? What do they value? How does knowing these things help you manage them?

- Was there a time when an unfounded rumor clouded your early impression of a team member? How should you have treated that rumor?

- What does one of your team members someday aspire to do or become? How does this aspiration impress you?

The West Pointer Gets to Know Team Members for their Capabilities

I remember, as a plebe, being convinced that the world was crashing down upon my shoulders. All the plebes in our company felt that way. There was just too much to do: deliver newspapers and laundry to the upperclass cadets, maintain some of the common areas, clean our rooms, polish our brass and our shoes, keep our uniforms in order, memorize plebe "poop," practice marching, complete homework for a twenty-credit semester, play sports.

After spinning our wheels for a few weeks, we eventually came to realize that we each carried strengths that—through cooperation—could help alleviate some of the stress. Some of us were good organizers, able to coordinate efficient groups of newspaper and laundry deliveries. Some of us were tidy cleaners, capable of quickly knocking out the area chores or taking care of our rooms. Others offered helpful hints to the group on keeping brass and shoes shined and uniforms crisp. Still others knew secrets for memorizing plebe knowledge and muscling through academic projects.

In time we became comfortable trading time and ability among the various obligations. It was the synergy of this cooperation that got us through a very difficult, time-pressed year.

The effective organizational leader knows the capacities of each team member. Furthermore, she knows the *potential* that each team member possesses. Once you have become familiar with the personalities of your team, it's time to learn about their task-related qualifications. You should assess each member's competence and determine if all of their competencies mesh. You should determine if there are gaps between team competencies and requirements.

Getting to know your team members' capabilities begins with clarifying the mission of the greater organization and how it relates to the mission of your team. You should find out if each team member is able to tell you what these missions are. That is, the individual members of your team should know what the big picture is and how they each fit into it. If there is not a written set of tasks for the team, you are in the unenviable position of having to create one. If machinery or some type of potential hazard is involved, a written set of safety standards needs to exist.

The effective organizational leader knows the capacities of each team member.

Next, determine what each team member does well. You should establish if these abilities form different pieces of the puzzle, and when you're done piecing them all together, if the puzzle is complete. If there are too many missing pieces, or if the missing pieces are huge, then either serious training is in order or you must switch out those people whose skills don't match the team assignment.

Discover your team's weaknesses, including what each team member does poorly. Don't be shy: test the proficiency of your team members. Ask them questions. Have them talk you through their workday, their chores, and their competencies. Let them demonstrate their skills.

Dylan Haas served in the military as an infantry officer, an Army Ranger, a general's aide-de-camp, and an operations officer serving foreign military staffs in South and Central America. He now works as an onsite engagement manager who travels throughout the world for McKinsey & Company, a management-consulting firm. Haas says that appraising one's team means taking inventory of their skills in an ongoing, dynamic way. "Make evaluation interesting for everyone," he offers. "Assign a task that you know will stretch a person's ability. Then watch to see how well he performs, and see what capabilities and skills show themselves. I'm often pleasantly surprised when the skill that emerges is not the reason the team member was initially brought on board."

Find out if there is a common task that everyone does poorly and if the team or the organization has suffered because of it. Establish how the team can train together to learn this shared requirement. Consider the possibility that the task, as defined, is outside the scope or the capacity of everyone on your team.

Assess the state of training at your organization and how your team members *perceive* the state of training. Look through the training plan if one exists. Find out from the members of your team if they find training interesting and worthwhile or if a call for training brings on a combined groan. There's no point in reinventing the wheel: if there's a good process in your organization for getting people taught and trained, and if your team members buy into it, then use it.

There's something of an art to picking the brains of your team members in order to gauge their capabilities. People may not want to let on how much they know, for fear of getting handed an unfair portion of the duties. A display of firmness and fairness might help allay these fears. Moreover, the inspirational leader sells all the team members on the importance of the mission, prompting people to *want* to contribute, to band together, and to offer all they can collectively to keep the objectives within reach.

Supply and production manager Rich Vincz suggests that capabilities are best assessed when they are quantified. "Get to know your team by looking at its measurable performance," he recommends. "Don't be intimidating during your scrutiny. But do establish what you're going to observe and stick around long enough to assess the skills your team has to work with."

Remember, not only should people's personalities mesh, but so should their capabilities. Their tasks should be compatible— even synergistic—if great things are to be accomplished.

FOR CONSIDERATION:

- What are the capabilities of each member on your team? What special talent does each person bring to the table?

- Does each member on your team hold the potential for carrying out an important required task? Can that potential be developed?

- Does your organization have a written set of tasks and standards? If not, how might you go about creating one?

- Do your team's skills mesh? Are there any gaps between the collective skills of your team and what needs to get done by the team?

The West Pointer Cherishes the Soldier

Gus Pagonis is the Senior Vice President of Logistics for Sears, Roebuck and Co. He is responsible for all the logistical aspects of Sears, including inventory management, transportation, distribution, and delivery. Twelve years prior, Pagonis worked a different logistics mission—keeping half a million U.S. soldiers in Operation Desert Storm clothed, fed, and well-armed. He was the commanding general of the 22nd Support Command in Saudi Arabia.

Pagonis recognizes a huge difference between low-level management in the military and in business. "In the Army, everything is centered on the private," he says. "The military cares deeply about the soldier. Unfortunately, the corporate world at large doesn't always focus on the lower-tiered employee. That's unfortunate, because concern for employees at all levels is just good business."

Pagonis is right. In the military, there is nothing more sacred than the morale, well-being, training, and safety of the lowest-ranked soldier. Even the drill sergeant, who spends his day dogging basic trainees and running them through the muck, cares for them a great deal.

It's no different at West Point, where plebes are mercilessly harangued, criticized, and challenged throughout the day. Eventually they figure out that it's all a bit of a game (albeit a serious one) and that, in fact, their well-being and professional development is the inner core around which the whole Academy world revolves. At the end of the day, nothing is more important to the officers and upperclass cadets of West Point than plebes asleep, in one piece, with a little learning and experience stuck in their brains.

In business, however, where the ultimate focus is on maximizing shareholder wealth and pleasing the board of directors, the lowest-level employees are sometimes ignored. It doesn't have to be that way—a notion that some flourishing corporations throughout the world have figured out. "It is possible and desirable to tie business success with caring for people in the process," says Dylan Haas. "Some of the most successful managers I've seen have bridged those two objectives."

Why does focusing on the lowest tier of employment make good business sense? First, it brings everyone into the mix and gets everyone to buy into the big-picture missions of the organization. As mentioned before, once everybody feels they own a part of the bigger vision, enthusiasm and unique talents combine to forward the cause.

Second, a strong structure needs a strong foundation, and the foundation of any company is its mass

Concern for employees at all levels is just good business.

of workers, the bottom of the pyramid, so to speak. Exciting and vibrant companies consistently demonstrate a solid force of motivated employees just above entry level.

Third, caring for all workers shows consideration for a myriad of corporate policies and government laws and regulations that state, in one form or another, "you'd better watch over your lambs." Many of today's employment laws originated, not in the minds of politicians looking to gain votes or endorsements, but in the policies of employers who blazed a trail for worker respect and well-being.

Finally, concentrating on all members of the team is an essential component to developing your company's future mid- and upper-tier leaders. Addressing the new hire as the company's future CEO instills the notion of worth in that employee, perhaps creating a long-term, self-fulfilling prophesy.

Esther Taitsman is the director of the Master of Science in Management program at Thomas Edison State College in

Trenton, New Jersey. She suggests that cherishing workers ultimately cultivates a support and motivation process that makes companies economically superior to their rivals. "Without a doubt, a competitive edge comes from dealing with workers on a very personal and individual level." She says that a "do unto others" mentality for any manager will be returned tenfold.

To be sure, there's a limit to all of this caring attention. After all, there is a mission to be performed and, at some point, soldiers are called to sacrifice. But the effort they put forth and the feeling of personal commitment and perseverance they feel will be largely influenced by the care and respect—directly or indirectly—they have been given leading up to this crucial point. Similarly, a company that depends upon its people during a critical time will have stored up a lot of credit by demonstrating an earlier concern for its employees.

FOR CONSIDERATION:

• How does your team care for its lowest-tier organizational members?

• What are the team benefits to addressing the needs of these lowest-tier members? What are the bottom-line benefits?

• How does one go about balancing the needs of the greater organization with the needs of the team members?

The West Pointer Listens and Writes Things Down

West Point cadets love to tell a story. I don't mean a lie, of course, or even a tall tale—but an extended, enthralling anecdote. Very often in our company lounge, the cadets of D-4, the Dukes, would tell stories about what happened to whom, and where, over the weekend, or how someone had managed to get into trouble or avoid getting into trouble. The funniest, gut-hurting stories I've ever heard came out of the Duke lounge. And many of my company mates worked very hard to top the story that had just been told. At the same time, the room always contained one or two people who remained silent. They would nod their heads, smile, and laugh with the rest of us, but these same people rarely chimed in with a story of their own.

Intriguingly, as people told their stories, they focused on these quiet listeners, as if drawn to their silence. Perhaps they were hoping for some sign of unspoken approval, or perhaps the storytelling best gravitated toward the people who weren't actively participating. My guess: the silence of these few classmates created an aura of authority, placing them almost above the fray as the festivities were taking place (almost like the Romans looking down on the frenzied feeding of the lions). Even more likely, their silence portrayed genuine interest, and people were lured by the attention. Finally, I suspect that the unspoken manner of these few people suggested a quiet intelligence—the work of an analytic mind absorbing and digesting the art of interesting storytelling.

Still waters run deep. And such it is with the quiet, pensive manner of the West Pointer—hushed, unruffled, and very much in tune with the surrounding world. West Pointers keep their senses sharply tuned to good things in progress and bad things brewing.

The West Pointer has made listening to others an art form, particularly when team members are speaking. When approached with a problem or concern, he nods his head, displays the courtesy of open concern, and writes it down. Is part of this action a performance for others? Sure. When people see him writing down their issue on a daily planner page among many other obligations, they a) respect his busy day, b) appreciate that he won't forget the topic as soon as he walks away, and c) perceive that the matter will at some point be addressed.

Isn't it fascinating how such a visual signal can impact a team? Good listening might be an art, but it should be treated like a science. To practice good listening means to display oneself as open to feedback. It means having good body language, like leaning forward in your chair when someone speaks, nodding your head, and using eye contact. It means keeping your mouth shut through the entire sentence of the person who's talking.

A West Pointer is a wonderful listener. Her Academy training has taught her how to sit down with a soldier and find out exactly what's on that soldier's mind. As a cadet, she was taught the listening technique of Carl Rogers, called client-centered therapy. It's a simple process, really, of repeating back to a person, or mirroring, what you have just heard. If you've heard it right, the person responds by continuing on and expanding. If you haven't offered back the problem correctly, or if the person feels like the critical point isn't coming across, the person will restate the point and move along. Not only is this technique a superb way to get someone to open up, but it also makes for effective self solution when the person hears the problem recited back. The end result is wonderful introspection and revelation.

Marc McCreery offers some advice for effective listening. First, he suggests that carrying a notepad, clipboard, or daily planner need not be for show only. Jotting down people's thoughts and concerns and then considering them and prioritizing them should be a daily part of any manager's workplace. It's a part of the managing-by-walking-around that hands-on leaders are accustomed to. "At least once a day, I try to grab a clipboard and walk the production line," he says. "Not only does it show people that management's listening, but it often produces very useful feedback on the process."

McCreery suggests another noticeable symbol of interest: following up with the person who approaches you with a concern. "Some people are nothing short of amazed when you return a day or two later to report on your progress," he notes. "You set yourself apart from most others when you come back to people and tell them the results of their feedback." The downside, he suggests, is that *everyone* might begin coming to you. The solution: make sure everybody starts a suggestion with their immediate supervisor. People from outside your team should approach you only when their own chains of command have shut them out.

> *Remove your subjectivity screens so that you can hear what a person is saying and not what you want the person to be saying.*

When listening to members of your team, look for the story behind the story. What people say and what they're trying to say, even subconsciously, might be different. Look for patterns in the concerns of several team members, signaling a bigger problem—perhaps an unspoken problem. Sift through the daily bellyaching and find the nuggets of information and, yes, advice that will help you to improve your team and the conditions they'll be working under as they push for victory. Management academic director Esther Taitsman notes that "too many people hear the words, but not the *intent* behind the words." She recommends that you try to remove your subjectivity screens so that you can hear what a person is saying and not what you *want* the person to be saying.

What's the bottom-line reason for listening intently to others? Do it because few other leaders do, because it gives you the edge with extra information, and because it shows your team that you care.

FOR CONSIDERATION:

- Who was the last person to listen intently to one of your suggestions? How did it make you feel? What was the result?

- What are the signs that someone is listening to you?

- How open do you make yourself to the concerns of others?

- Do you write down suggestions? How do you organize them?

- When was the last time you followed up with someone regarding a concern?

The West Pointer Monitors Skills Training

General Douglas MacArthur (Class of 1903 and West Point Superintendent from 1919 to 1922) once said, "In no other profession are the penalties for employing untrained personnel so apparent or so irrevocable as in the military." People's lives are at stake, and so the leader takes a special interest in how training is envisioned, planned, implemented, and evaluated. However, the effectiveness of well-planned training suggests it has a significant place in any organization. Yes, leaders would prefer their team members to show up already trained and ready for the task, but the task is ever changing, and the world moves at a fast pace. Left to themselves, your team's abilities can quickly reach obsolescence. The solution: individual and team training, to include dynamic planning and cross-training of skills.

As a U.S. artillery platoon leader during Operation Desert Storm, I found myself in a unique training situation. My platoon was given orders to use its cannons offensively during an eighty-mile overland attack, after training for years to set up cannons in defensive positions (in other words, to protect territory). Fortunately, our platoon was well-trained and full of innovative ideas. Working with our battery's other cannon platoon and adhering to the guidelines our battalion and battery commanders gave us, we put together a creative method for traveling across the desert, stopping on a dime, and firing onto enemy targets. Had our previous training methods been stagnant, conceiving such a plan might have been tedious or impossible.

It is worth mentioning that I didn't simply assign the training and walk away. Effective leaders are always on hand. Sticking around and immersing oneself in skills training lets the team know that the information is important and that, following a session of training, the leader fully understands the nature of the tasks.

The tenth West Point Principle of Leadership is, "Train your soldiers as a team."

Make sure they're learning not only how to perform certain skills, but how to use them as a team. If the job requires a level of synchronization, make sure their timing matches the dance. If the job requires synergy, make certain these different tasks merge in such a way to produce a cohesive result. Such training should be multi-echelon, where training is happening on an individual level, a sub-team level, and a team level—all at the same time. The tasks being taught could range from as physical as operating new pieces of construction machinery to as cerebral as running new computer software.

Any good training program begins with reinforcing the things the team should already know. A combined job description review helps the leader compile a list of what people should know individually and collectively. Take a thorough inventory of what it is your team knows, as compared to what you hoped they *already* knew.

The key part of training is learning something new—preferably something new and functional. The things that your team members need to learn can be deduced through their feedback, through your boss's feedback, and through your knowledge of upcoming missions. It doesn't hurt to read about developments in your field. Also, talk to your colleagues and ask what their teams are learning. Even competitors are open with each other about training, particularly training that's done right.

Training should be laser-focused on ridding the team of its weaknesses. It should serve as the cement that repairs the crack. When a team is finished training, its members should feel confident about their team's expertise and their individual expertise. Training should solve questions and restore confidence. If it exacerbates questions and causes anxiety, then a) the training wasn't taught correctly, b) the training didn't match the weakness, or c) everything went fine, but a new weakness was revealed in the process. Make adjustments, and push forward again. And stick around!

What's the best part about a West Pointer being on hand for skills training?

Effective leaders are always on hand.

It reminds him that training is never, ever as easy as it looks, that the tasks at hand are more intricate than one might think, and that there's a lot more forgotten than anyone initially thought. President Dwight D. Eisenhower (West Point Class of 1915) once said, "Farming looks mighty easy when your plow is a pencil, and you're a thousand miles from the corn field."

FOR CONSIDERATION:

- What skills among your team members could become obsolete soon? How might you respond early to the outmoding of these abilities?

- What skills does your team need to brush up on? Are any of them safety-related?

- Are there any gaps in your team's collective ability? What training might fill those gaps?

- What was the last skill-training class you sat in on as a leader? What was the team's response to your presence? Did you learn anything?

- What skills on your team involve several people doing things in order or at the same time? How might you go about training for such complex tasks?

- What is the source of your team's training? After visiting a training session, were you happy with the trainer? Why or why not?

The West Pointer Knows that the Soldier is the Smartest Member of the Team

Dylan Haas tells a funny story about a weapons training site where his unit trained. An ammunitions truck stopped and soldiers were ordered to unload the boxes of ammo and stack them in the ordnance shed, about three hundred feet away. Two squads of soldiers jumped to the task, unloading the heavy boxes and passing them, in a water-bucket line, over to the shed. A minute or two later, the newest private in the platoon asked, "Sir, would it be okay if we just moved the truck up to the shed?" Everyone stopped, looked at each other, and smiled that "happens-all-the-time" smile. In a training area reasonably populated with officers and sergeants, a young, straight-out-the-wrapper soldier had, once again, offered the commonsense solution of the day. The truck was moved to the shed.

It's understandable why the soldier, at times, is the "smartest" person on the team: a unit's newest members haven't yet had their

A good leader is open to good ideas— wherever they come from.

minds clouded with years of failures, worries, cynicism, and office politics. They see the world as sometimes it should be seen: through the lenses of optimism and simplicity. Sometimes, the best answer—the "smartest" answer—is also the easiest. The newest member of your team might just have a clear enough mind to spot it and recommend it—if you're listening.

The opinion of the soldier might also be more valuable than anyone realizes because of where that soldier stands: on the front line. If you're guarding a perimeter, it's better to get your information from the people on the outside than on the inside. Similarly, if you run a manufacturing facility, don't shy away from the observations of the people on your assembly lines.

Verizon teaches a corporate philosophy called "the shadow up," where the experience and innovations of team members impact the decisions made by higher-ups. The West Pointer appreciates this philosophy: he knows that the best ideas regularly come from the soldier on "point" who clearly sees the terrain ahead.

Are the assertions of these subordinates blindly believed and are their suggestions blindly gone along with? No. It's understood that everyone has something of a personal agenda, and opinions need to be gathered at several levels before charging forward. But to respect the soldier enough to pay attention to his opinion is to accept the possibility that perhaps, today, he's the smartest member of the team.

Dylan Haas observes, "A good manager maintains a degree of humility and openness about needing help. Common sense might suggest that breakthrough ideas come from people with a high level of experience. But a good leader is open to good ideas—wherever they come from."

Marc McCreery adds, "In many ways, everyone on the team is an equal—all the same. We each bring something equally important to the party."

FOR CONSIDERATION:

- Do you remember a time when someone new to the team, surprisingly, had the best idea of the day? How did you respond?

- What sometimes makes the best solution so obvious to the "new guy?"

- Do you generally trust the opinions and suggestion of people you supervise?

- What creates a situation where leaders mistrust their team members? What causes teams to mistrust their leaders?

- How could you be more open to ideas from the least likely sources?

CHAPTER SIX

EXECUTION

LET YOUR ACTIONS
DEFINE YOU AND INFLUENCE OTHERS

West Pointers Let Their Deeds Define Them

West Point cadets are taught a wide assortment of social skills, from how to eat properly using a knife and a fork to how to respond appropriately to a dinner party invitation. The knife, for example, gets canted on the plate along the upper-right edge of the plate when not being used and when one is chewing. Proper poise, listening skills, and respect toward others are all instilled so that any cadet becomes adept at "working a room." Ironically, the more a cadet becomes practiced in social and political skills at the Academy, the more he or she realizes how little these tools matter. Sure, every class at West Point has cadets that are the center of attention—kind of like the "big man (or woman) on campus" at any college.

But in every way imaginable, cadets are evaluated and ranked based on their quantifiable performance rather than on how they present themselves socially. Their physical training, or PT, scores—push-ups, sit-ups, and a two-mile run—count toward an academic grade. And their academic grade-point averages count toward where they are ranked among their other classmates—a standing that determines how many officer jobs each has to choose from, as well as how many places in the world each cadet can select for his or her first assignment. Put bluntly, cadets are judged and compared from Reception Day to Graduation Day on their deeds rather than on their words or social prowess.

This results-oriented philosophy carries into the new officer's first assignment and often lasts a lifetime. However, rather than seeking to "punch the ticket" with a series of high-profile exploits, the successful officer often follows a different course— the self-effacing path of small but plentiful acts that exhibit skill and dependability. The thriving long-term leader is often defined by consistent, reliable performance rather than loud, empty assertions.

When I was in the Army, I heard an old story about a rugged soldier who stirs the embers of the campfire while others sit around the fire and tell tall tales of self-proclaimed fearlessness and accomplishment. Although the quiet soldier offers no such stories, the others respect him just the same. After all, he's stirring the hot embers with his bare hand! The steely warrior in this anecdote can stay silent because his immediate actions overshadow the questionable claims of the braggarts. Quiet and sure—that's the way many unspoken heroes gain respect and influence.

During my time in the Army, I also learned that the best warriors were the most unlikely candidates. Many times, when people were expecting the loud, squared-jawed soldier to step forward during a difficult mission, it was the rumpled, ungainly soldier who surprised everyone by not only taking charge of a situation but also performing well under intense pressure. We all tend to be, at times, mesmerized by the tall, well-groomed, compelling executive who can command a room. But such charisma without genuine caring, wisdom, and personal accomplishment fades quickly, and people are left disillusioned by the reality.

For those people who still would rather define themselves with empty promises and office gamesmanship than with achievement, there's plenty of opportunity in any workplace. Just go to the nearest staff meeting and sit in on the antics. The conference room is the ultimate amusement center, as meetings often have little to do with reality. Each meeting has its own predictable cast of characters preoccupied with their own images and self-serving agendas. The shame of it is that such behavior is often endorsed and supported by the organization, and such unproductive meeting time is often mistaken for achievement.

That's not to say leaders shouldn't be concerned about their image. There is really nothing wrong with self-promotion. In fact, sometimes there's nothing wrong with *shameless* self-promotion. But a good leader understands that a strong image must have the backing of skill and integrity and that, sometimes, the reticent but accomplished leader is the loudest self-advocate in the office.

For those people who would rather define themselves with empty promises and office gamesmanship than with achievement, there's plenty of opportunity in any workplace.

Music industry licensing and copyright director Leah Gebhardt notes that when people define themselves through their deeds, they tend to be taken at their word, and their promises are accepted as certainties. "If someone has a habit of quietly completing tasks, then you have a good feeling that future work—important work—will be delivered."

Effective businesspeople define themselves with accomplishments and dependability—not with empty words and staff meeting fluff.

FOR CONSIDERATION:

- Have you ever discovered an impressive, unspoken accomplishment of someone you thought you knew well? How did you react?

- How do people who define themselves through their deeds overshadow those who attempt to characterize themselves with words?

- What effect does the quiet, successful leader have on the team?

- Is your organization preoccupied with conference-room posturing or office politics?

- Have you ever been surprised by the capable performance of someone you thought couldn't do the job? What happened?

The West Pointer Sets the Example

By most accounts, plebes today have it a lot better than the plebes of twenty years ago. Although I never went through the wringer like the poor West Pointers of the early 1900s, I sustained enough hazing in the mid-1980s, under the discipline configuration known as the Fourth-Class System, to boast about completing a year-long rite of passage. There were enough dinners when the senior cadets at the table kept me busy serving drinks and going through all sorts of silly gyrations, yelling the entire time and thus preventing me from eating. I would later squeeze half a tube of toothpaste into my mouth just to put some bulk in my stomach. I went through a few disciplinary boards where I stood at attention before upperclass cadets sitting in a dark room at a table with lit candles and crossed sabers, and I received some unofficial forms of punishment (unscheduled time walking "the area" with a rifle, extra work duty, scrubbing areas not normally cleaned by cadets). I was made to stand at attention at length in the rooms of first-class cadets who talked endlessly about how they were going to run me out, speaking nose to nose and spraying my face with each pointed word. And I was convinced that a handful of first-class cadets hated me more than anyone else and would someday snap and thrash me.

And so, it was with great anticipation that I waited for Role Reversal Night, the one evening toward the end of Plebe Year when, in the time between dismissal from dinner and Call to Quarters, the plebes were allowed to assume the role of firsties and the senior cadets were supposed to brace themselves at attention, crank their necks back against the hallway walls, and play the part of plebes. The first-class cadets, sensing our anticipation, made things especially hard on us the week leading up to Role Reversal, which in turn heightened our expectation.

As it turned out, when the evening of Role Reversal came around and we were set free to hunt the firsties, many of them had left for the "firstie club," a bar for seniors only that was nowhere near the barracks. And of those who stayed around, only a few stood at attention and pretended to be plebes.

There were, however, a few firsties who came out of their rooms with their uniforms neatly pressed and their shoes spit-shined to mirrors. They stood at attention and braced against the walls and did their best to recite "plebe knowledge." One such firstie was Cadet Captain Warren Wintrode. Emerging from his room with a perfect uniform and thick, black, military-issue glasses, Wintrode played the role of plebe to perfection, almost as if he had been carried back in time to his own fourth-class year. Clearly, he had prepared for this evening and had studied his "knowledge." Several of us stood in front of him, hoping to trip him up.

"Wintrode, how many gallons of water are there in Lusk Reservoir?"

"Seventy-eight million gallons, sir, when the water is flowing over the spillway."

"What's the poop, Wintrode?"

"Sir, today in the *New York Times*, it was reported that..."

"What's Schofield's Definition of Discipline, Wintrode?"

"Sir, Schofield's Definition of Discipline: 'The discipline which makes the soldiers of a free country reliable in battle is not to be gained by harsh or tyrannical treatment. On the contrary, such treatment is far more likely to destroy than to make an army...'"

"Wintrode, what's the second verse of 'The 'Star-Spangled Banner'?"

"Sir, the second verse of 'The Star-Spangled Banner': 'Oh, thus be it ever when free men shall stand between their loved homes and wild war's desolation...'"

We couldn't trip him up. He stood there for a couple of hours, taking all the heat that was given to him and spouting out endless minutia he hadn't been required to know for three years. I dare say that by the end of the evening, we were more rattled than he was!

When Call to Quarters was sounded over the speaker system and the roles were restored once again, Warren Wintrode left the wall, removed the dorky glasses, and hazed us ("I'm going to light you smacks like cigars!") on our way back to our rooms.

Wintrode's masterful plebe performance that night prompted me, three years later, to study my plebe knowledge and *Leading by example has turned many a leader into a transformational leader.* attempt a similar presentation when the roles were reversed, although I doubt if I did nearly as well. Wintrode had put the fourth-class system into a clear light, making me understand that, although it was all just something of a game, it had a purpose and had to be played capably. I suspect I treated plebes more professionally during my latter three years as a cadet, in part, because of Wintrode's inspiring example that evening.

Leading by example has turned many a leader into a transformational leader, prompting the team to follow the model they've been given. Setting the example can take your team to greater heights.

FOR CONSIDERATION:

- Have you ever had a boss who made it a habit to set the example? What sort of impact did this method of leadership have on you?

- When was the last time you set the example for someone on your team? What happened?

- Why does setting the example have such a strong impact on the team?

- What difficulties come with setting the example? Why doesn't every manager set the example?

The West Pointer Gets Dirty

In his great leadership book *The Rogue Warrior's Strategy for Success,* Richard Marcinko tells a wonderful anecdote about World War II icon George Patton (West Point Class of 1909). The story goes that the famous tank commander came upon some of his staff looking over maps, trying to determine where best to cross a river. Patton pointed at the map. "Cross here." Patton's staff hesitated, claiming they didn't know how deep the water was at that spot.

Patton pointed at his wet pants, drawing attention to the waterline. "It's this deep," he said.

Never one for diplomacy or keeping up appearances, Patton was known and beloved by his troops for leading with a "follow me" attitude, as his Third Army stunned the Nazis, pushing them out of France and back into Germany. In sum, he believed in getting dirty—moving among the soldiers and shouting war cries to keep them focused on the mission of driving forward.

If there ever was a time in human history when commanding from behind the line of combat made sense, then that time surely is gone. The notion of officers enjoying tea time while their soldiers engage in battle is a far cry from today's reality. With the world turning its attention to low-intensity urban warfare, having leadership close at hand is not only good for morale, but it's essential for command and control. Such a perspective starts with training: when soldiers are low crawling in the mud in a "training lane," it's not unusual to see their lieutenant creeping alongside them, encouraging them every mucky foot of the way.

Much the same can be said for how a manager should act in the aggressive, ever-changing world of business. While people don't necessarily expect or desire their supervisors to always be around, they surely hold an aversion for the one who prefers to manage solely from the glass fortress of an office. "Getting dirty" doesn't just apply to physical jobs. Getting dirty means getting involved, being on hand, and understanding the issues of the moment. It means occasionally offering to do menial work like helping the team pour over records or put together a report. It means helping someone—even for a few minutes— move into an office or over to a new office. It means staying late with the team when a project *has* to get done.

Besides having a good handle on what's going on, there's another reason to "get dirty" with your team: people appreciate it. They know that their boss doesn't *really* have to be in the trenches and that it's perfectly acceptable for bosses to hand out work direction and then get lost in meetings and long lunches. However, the boss who is on hand, asking questions, offering assistance—without nit-picking or micromanaging—is valued as someone who cares enough to be around and is smart enough to stay abreast of what's going on.

When I was a production shift supervisor at International Paper in the mid-1990s, our paper mill started making a paper product requiring a very thick mix, or "heavy stock." The mill had to refurbish and restart a very old dewatering machine involving a giant turning roll and a weir. Put simply, wood fiber and water were brought into a tub. The wood fiber stuck to the turning roll and the water was channeled away. The dewatered fiber was removed from the roll by a long, thin wedge called a "doctor blade."

> *The astute business leader understands the phrase "where the rubber meets the road." He's the one with gravel and tire marks on his business suit!*

To keep the mechanism working for long periods, the doctor blade had to be monitored with a small amount of water keeping it clear and preventing the thick stock from backing up.

It was an art rather than a science, playing with the water pressure and the distance of the doctor blade to the turning roll.

Many times, I watched my crew tend the machine, having to unplug the thick stock because something wasn't exactly right. And by the time the system was working again, we would all walk away completely covered in paper stock. If nothing else, they knew I understood how temperamental that old contraption could be.

The astute business leader understands the phrase "where the rubber meets the road." He's the one with gravel and tire marks on his business suit!

FOR CONSIDERATION:

- Do you appreciate a boss who likes to be "where the rubber meets the road"?

- Why do you suppose some bosses avoid being around their teams?

- Why might hands-on management be effective in a fast-paced, fluid situation?

- Has there been a time recently when hands-on management helped you handle a situation quickly and effectively? What happened?

The West Pointer Makes Others Care Without Ordering Them To Do So

People generally do not change unless they internalize a problem and its solution. Convincing people of the important need to initiate improvements makes the good solution a hundred times more likely.

Marshall O. Larsen, West Point Class of 1970, is chairman, president, and CEO of Goodrich, Inc. Initially famous for its tire making, Goodrich has become much more influential in recent history as a global aerospace corporation. Although Larsen took the helm in 2003, he was part of the senior leadership that had to confront the financial crisis faced by airlines and related companies following the terrorist attacks of September 11, 2001. "If it wasn't for hiring great people before the crisis—people we could count on for innovation and resilience—the tough ride following September 11 would have been a lot tougher," he says. As the airlines worked to improve security, and as consumers began the long process of becoming comfortable with flying again, a parked fleet of one thousand to two thousand airplanes translated into a dramatic reduction in airplane orders. Goodrich, with business units in aircraft electronic systems, airframe systems, and engine systems, faced a big hit. "Over the five quarters following 9/11, we shut down twenty facilities," Larsen notes. "In a business as complex as this one, you can't just put a chain across a door. You have to scale back in a way that still allows an integrated set of teams to get their job done, and allows for growth once the situation turns itself around."

Larsen remembers the days immediately following the attacks. "We had to dramatically revise our one-year business plan in light of those events. But rather than forcing a new plan onto our people, we tapped into their commonsense ideas and their opinions, considering all of them—including the dissenting ones. We also gathered lots of people together and explained to them that the short-term goals were maintaining cash liquidity on hand, setting important new cash-flow objectives, and successfully continuing orders still in the pipeline."

Larsen emphasizes the significance of not laying out a hard-and-fast strategy from the start. "Our purpose early on was getting people to buy into the objective of preservation and crisis management. As our plan incorporated many of the ideas of others, having the team buy into the overall objectives was easier than if we had charted a strict path for everyone to follow. Once the team recognized its own contributions to this plan, it became very committed toward the common good of the company."

By embracing and adopting ideas submitted by team members, the leader can count on a solution that includes team involvement and approval.

Larsen says the approach helped to create a situation where people cared deeply about their mission. The method also meant harvesting a better selection of good initiatives to choose from. "It got to the point where we regularly asked 'How can we do this?' and had wonderful ideas come back to us." The company created several strategies for weathering through the adversity, such as an incentive system for business units that met their cash-flow objectives.

At the moment, Goodrich is receiving increased orders for airplane systems again. "We are largely out of the storm," Larsen says. And he says the company will keep its method of pulling people aside—sometimes for a day or two at a time—and collecting ideas.

The great leader commands a team that genuinely cares about its future and the triumph of its missions. By embracing and adopting ideas submitted by team members, the leader can count on a solution that includes team involvement and approval.

FOR CONSIDERATION:

- Trying to make someone "care" about something seems as unlikely as forcing him or her to love another person. How might it be possible to persuade someone to really care about a team priority or team objective?

- How might it be possible to channel people's attention away from their anxiety over a crisis and instead get them to focus on addressing and solving the crisis?

- What are the benefits of seeking ideas from the team at large?

The West Pointer Is Sometimes Hated, But Always Respected

The West Pointer is not always beloved. In fact, by serving as a passionate advocate for the team, the cause, the worker, or even the truth, he is essentially choosing sides. And by taking any sort of stand, this leader invariably creates enemies. Taking a firm position not only sets a leader apart from those on the opposing side of the argument, but it distinguishes him from those in the organization who would rather not take any position at all. Large organizations often foster the misconception that quietly walking the line down the middle of the road can carry a person a long way for a long time. The strong, opinionated manager is sometimes problematic for a stagnant organization that cherishes the status quo or the blind eye. Sometimes, that manager is downright hated.

I recall, as a cadet, hearing the superintendent of the Academy, Lieutenant General Willard W. Scott Jr., tell the story of a few German soldiers in World War II who refused to take part in firing squad exercises, declaring that the civilians they were being asked to execute had done nothing wrong. The reward for this noble stand was to be stripped of their weapons and uniforms and forced to position themselves alongside the very people they had spoken up for. As other soldiers replaced them in the firing squad, these high-minded men were put to death. "They instantly were vilified for taking the moral stance," said Scott. "Let us hope they reaped their reward as souls in another place."

Although life does not always serve up such dramatic, life-and-death, good-versus-evil choices for us to pick from, we as managers are often faced with taking the rigid view that runs against the grain. A good friend of mine (whom I first met at West Point as a cadet) is now a vice president in a giant investment trust company. He remembers, some years ago, being a part of a large merger that—after a round of consolidations and lay-offs—resulted in his promotion. He was, at that point, the only vice president to come from the acquired company, and at thirty-three, the youngest VP by at least ten years. He now oversaw $400 million in sales as part of an organization with four thousand employees. "All the other vice presidents had worked together for years and were much more experienced than I was," he says.

During a meeting with the senior leadership, my friend listened as the president of the company was briefed on a major investment deal involving a company preparing to sell a new type of medical kit throughout the world. The investment was projected to net the company millions of dollars in profit each year. However, when asked for feedback from the group, my friend hesitantly spoke up. "My concern," he recalls, "was that the way these kits were being distributed would mean that they would fall into the hands of people without medical training. I felt that, on balance, more people throughout the world would wind up hurting themselves as they substituted these kits for proper medical care." The sale was legal and did not violate any United States or international law, and the company's connection to the deal freed them from any liability. There were no possible negative repercussions—just the moral question of whether or not it was right to finance the international distribution of these medical kits.

Be comfortable with your method, and people will respect your outlook.

Needless to say, there was much discussion at that meeting, and my friend's view was not embraced. "Sure, I felt the heat," he admits, "but my argument was that one of our goals was to convince our employees that they were involved in more than just a job, that our corporation was concerned with more than just turning profits. Without considering moral issues, I felt like we were turning our backs on that goal."

The issue was eventually decided by the president, the CEO, and the major owners of the corporation. They chose not to pursue the project. "I'm not sure if I was loved after that one," says my friend, "but I believed I earned their respect."

"Everyday stressful situations are leadership laboratories," he observes. "You're sometimes going to be disliked for the tough stands—the strong decision mixtures you concoct. The key is to be comfortable with your method and your blends, and people will respect your outlook."

People don't always cheer and support the leader who arrives with strong opinions, rigid standards, and upright morals. But they always respect such a leader, and eventually come to understand that such a presence is good for the organization.

FOR CONSIDERATION:

- Have you ever taken a tough stand that others in your organization hated, but which you knew in your heart was right?

- Have you ever begrudgingly respected a team leader even though you "hated" the decision that leader was making?

- Is it okay to sometimes be "hated" for your rigid standards or your tough stances?

The West Pointer Understands
the Power of Symbolism

As West Point changes with the times—often against the wishes of the Long Gray Line's living graduates—some traditions stay around forever. One of those traditions is a tough academic curriculum, responsible for expelling more cadets from the Academy than all of the physical and psychological challenges combined. Another lasting tradition is the cadet's secret weapon for passing the exam of a particularly difficult course.

West Point graduate John Sedgwick was a Union general in the Civil War, the son of a famous Revolutionary War general of the same name. Part of his historical prominence is attributed to his never having lost a battle. He led troops at Bull Run and at Antietam, where legend suggests that two different horses he rode were shot dead during the fierce fighting. His arrival with troops from the 6th Army Corps at Gettysburg is credited with helping to turn the campaign in favor of the Union troops. At Spottslvania, where he was giving directions to the artillery, he suggested aloud to his cannon troops that they were positioned so far away from the enemy line that "they couldn't hit an elephant at this distance"—at which point he was shot dead by a Confederate sniper! And yet his troops still were triumphant in that battle.

There is a statue of General Sedgwick at West Point, reputedly cast from a Confederate cannon captured by the 6th Corps. A few years ago, the statue was moved to the Plain by the main parade bleachers, but when I was a cadet, it was intermingled with other monuments at Trophy Point, overlooking the winding Hudson River. On the boots of the statue are the actual spurs that Sedgwick wore when he was shot down at Spottslvania, and the rowels of the spurs spin freely on the bronze boots. For the Corps of Cadets, those spurs symbolize the Sedgwick tradition of victory—victory that carries all the way to one's death. On the midnight before a make-or-break final exam, tradition dictates that if a cadet—in parade full-dress uniform—sneaks out, salutes General Sedgwick, spins the rowels of the spurs, and returns to the barracks without being caught, he or she will pass the exam and the course.

It was in the spring of my junior, or "cow," year that I experienced lots of difficulty with an engineering course called ME304 Thermofluid Dynamics. I had been failing the entire semester and needed something of a miracle on the final exam to avoid retaking the course in cadet summer school. I decided to put General Sedgwick in my corner. My roommate Eric Keltz watched me throw on my brass and belts. "Uh, don't you think your time would be better utilized if you spent it studying?" he asked teasingly.

"I've been studying all night. Besides, what if the myth is true? Why put myself at a disadvantage by *not* going?"

Once in parade full-dress, I snuck out of the barracks, ran past the superintendent's house, and made my way to Trophy Point. Twice, I flattened myself against the ground as the military police rode by. Trophy Point was off-limits at night, and cadets were supposed to be in their quarters. When I reached General Sedgwick, I was surprised—but shouldn't have been—to find a line of cadets with the same idea as mine! A few moments later, I took my turn. Saluting the statue: "Sir, request permission to spin your spurs." I spun the rowels and made my way back to the barracks.

A few days later, the grades were posted. A course grade of 60 was required to pass with a D. My grade was a 60.7, the third lowest passing score that semester. It would be my only D and my only serious brush with failing at the Academy. General Sedgwick had come through!

There's probably little more to the Sedgwick legend than carrying a good luck charm or keeping one's fingers crossed. But to the extent that perhaps a cadet is more relaxed or confident taking an exam after visiting the statue, the symbolism is powerful and effective. The West Pointer carries the dramatic lesson of symbolism past graduation and uses it frequently to convey a message. An example would be a commander who carves a notch on a walking stick whenever a mission is successfully completed. When the commander shows up carrying a stick with hundreds of notches on it, no one wants to be the one who keeps that stick from gaining another notch.

NFL coach Bill Parcells, who led the New York Giants to two Super Bowl titles, later on coached the New York Jets to the AFC East championship. While watching over his playoff season practices, he prominently wore one of his Super Bowl rings for his players to notice. The symbolism was authoritative: You *can* be a winner; it is within your reach.

And so it is also with the beloved West Point school ring, a monster-sized hunk of gold and stones that cadets are allowed to purchase and wear their senior year. These somewhat garish ornaments serve as powerful symbols to the younger classes. *Hang in there for three years and you can put on the ring. Hang in there for four and you can wear it out of here.*

The power of symbolism is that it draws out positive emotions, which might give the team a competitive edge. Military examples include uniform garb (symbols of attainment), medals (symbols of achievement), and unit or country flags (symbols of belonging). A headquarters or main body serves as an important symbol for the entire organization. An example is the Continental Army during the Revolutionary War. Although the state militias contributed more to the cause of independence, the existence of the Continental Army and the British Army's failure to destroy it served as an inspiring symbol of patriot resolve. And, certainly, the team leader—George Washington—was the personified symbol of the cause itself.

These symbols can be converted to any organization. For example, rather than offering medals, an organization can openly reward and encourage good performance with published announcements of achievement, time off, and pay bonuses.

Symbolism doesn't have to be loud and flashy. The understated symbolism of a written thank-you note from a supervisor, for example, is very powerful in conveying appreciation on a personal level. The body language associated with listening skills—a nodding head as the listener leans forward—also serves as a very encouraging, yet unassuming, symbol of concern or approval.

> *Rather than offering medals, an organization can openly reward and encourage good performance with published announcements of achievement, time off, and pay bonuses.*

The good leader understands that people are affected not only by words and actions, but also by the symbols—both overt and subtle—that surround them.

FOR CONSIDERATION:

- What are the prominent symbols used by people in your organization? What do they symbolize? Do they work?

- What are some of the less conspicuous symbols used by successful managers in your organization? What do they symbolize? Do they work?

- Why are symbols potentially effective management tools?

CHAPTER SEVEN

STRATEGY

UNDERSTAND THE SECRET OF
GOOD TACTICS AND GOOD TIMING

The West Pointer Understands the Terrain and the Clock

Making the right decisions doesn't always win the battle. Sometimes, doing so involves making the right decisions at the *right times*. Early on during their time at West Point, cadets are taught how to look at an operation from several different dimensions, how to put it in the context of other things going on at the time, and how to do the right thing at a time when it will have the most beneficial effect.

Camp Buckner is a wooded area on the greater military installation that is West Point but removed from the Revolutionary War fortress that makes up the main campus of the Academy. During the summer at Camp Buckner directly after plebe year—the so-called "best summer of your life"—cadet field training for the new yearlings includes a series of classes and tests involving the proper reading and following of a map. I'm not talking about a road map—that folded sheet of paper that men stubbornly refuse to look at just before they refuse to ask directions. I'm talking about a military map, with terrain features such as streams, hilltops, ridges, and cliffs depicted through colors, symbols, and contour lines. Navigating a large area on foot with such a map takes talent and practice. When the stopwatch starts ticking, a new aspect to the challenge is added: the cadet is required to find and gather a certain number of land markers—chits left at the base of small flags—in a limited amount of time. The challenge for the cadet is to determine, while on the go, which route might lead to the most markers in the shortest amount of time. As one might expect, the easiest flags to find at the most distinguishable landmarks are located the farthest apart. The not-so-easy-to-find flags are closer together, but if the cadet gets lost trying to find this tighter landmark cluster, time easily runs out. The key is sizing up the nature of the terrain, letting the obvious landmarks— such as ponds, streams, or hilltops—become a giant frame of reference, and formulating a time-conscious course with a nice mix of difficult and easy markers. If a route is not going well, smart decision-making comes into play as the cadet decides whether or not to continue looking or move on to the next marker or to rethink the route entirely.

Some yearlings come back in no time at all, with more than the number of required markers. Others come back late, covered with sweat, grime, mud, and pieces of undergrowth, and possessing too few markers. Some never come back, and a search party ensues! (They're all found eventually, only to train some more and run the test again.)

Cadets who become very good at timed land navigation are encouraged to join West Point's *orienteering* team. Orienteering began as a competitive sport in Sweden in the early 1900s. It involves a map, a compass, and control points throughout a wooded area, meant for competitors with good cardiovascular fitness and a passion for reading, discerning, and racing with a map. Not surprisingly, the Academy consistently fields one of the best orienteering teams in the United States.

The lessons that come out of land navigation training extend past knowing how to read a military map. Cadets learn not to wander into any area, figuratively speaking, without first studying the map and understanding the terrain. In other words, they learn to determine what they're getting into, and the importance of thinking through and charting a course, one with enough flexibility to allow for intelligent midstream

Stay flexible and don't be afraid to change course.

changes. They learn how to maximize their time, not only through good time management, but also by channeling the most energy toward the best control point at the best time. Such lessons have nothing to do with team interaction or managing external resources: they involve only the personal, rational development of each cadet. And yet they are very important leadership lessons that remain with each cadet long after graduation.

The lessons of the terrain and the calendar are pretty straightforward. Examine your "map" first, taking in the big picture and then scrutinizing each grid. If other information is available regarding the terrain, including the experiences of others, tap into it.

Second, gauge your time requirement. Plan your time *backwards,* starting with the final objective and measuring each segment of time back to each prior control point. Add up the segments of time, then subtract the minutes from your planned time of arrival.

Third, double everything. Estimate your difficulty in navigating the terrain, then double the level of trouble and plan for this new level. Double your estimated time requirement and redo your timeline accordingly. You can never go wrong assuming any objective is twice as difficult and takes twice as long as initially anticipated.

Fourth, take the linear aspect out of your plan. That is, modify your plan so that the most urgent tasks get the most upfront, fresh energy and so that as many tasks are grouped together as possible. If there's synergy in combining two or more objectives, then combine them.

Fifth, plan your escape routes and your points of assessment. Do you know at what points you will evaluate your success and decide to continue, adjust, or bail out (if that's an option)?

Sixth, plan and take inventory of your resources before taking off into the woods. Do you have the necessities on hand to get you through the course? Is your "compass" working?

And finally, as you embark on your journey, stay flexible and don't be afraid to change course in the middle of your trip. Plodding along a path toward failure is the action of a failed manager. Accepting that things aren't going well and adjusting your direction are the actions of a strong-minded, dynamic leader.

Alan Shephard is a commercial contract salesman in the heating and air-conditioning business. He regularly offers bids to businesses for their heating maintenance and energy management projects. He has a recommendation for those who do not like the terrain once they become familiar with it: change it! "For example," he says, "if I possess expertise and reputation in a particular market, I can go about the business of altering what it is that potential customers are going to be interested in. If my competitors are emphasizing price but I have the better service, I'm going to draw attention to the service and win the business. At that point I have, in essence, changed the terrain while navigating it."

Every leader's journey requires a "map," a "compass," and a "stopwatch." The smart leader learns early on how to use these tools for timely navigation.

FOR CONSIDERATION:

- What does "knowing the terrain" mean to you as a team leader?

- What successes have you had in planning a journey for your team?

- What successes have you had in planning a timeline for your team?

- What successes have you had in taking inventory for a team journey?

- Describe what makes a plan appropriately flexible.

The West Pointer Makes Sound, Calculated Predictions

At some point, the bold leader must make predictions and decisions based on as much solid information and advice as possible.

At Camp Buckner, the new yearlings are introduced to the modern-day Field Artillery—long-range cannons and rockets—and are taught about the benefits of fire support. That is, if you're an infantry platoon leader and your platoon is facing a tough enemy, you can radio for fire support, call in the enemy's position, and let the artillery suppress the enemy. Effective use of fire support means predicting where the enemy will be positioned or headed, the size of your opponent's forces, and the type of fire that might best keep the enemy pinned down. As an enlisted soldier prior to attending West Point, and as a lieutenant following my time at the Academy, I was part of the U.S. Field Artillery. I remember sitting on an overlook, calling map coordinates over the radio, and, moments later, watching fire and steel rain down on that spot. Whether I was the forward observer calling in the fire or the cannon platoon leader sending the rounds downrange, the feeling was one of force and control.

Interestingly, the principles of fire support can just as easily be applied to business or to sensible decision-making in general. These principles involve making sound, calculated predictions and using those predictions to one's advantage. Making bold calculations—and, I should add, bold corrections—was part of what made this branch of service intriguing and rewarding.

The principles of fire support include planning your actions early. The planning process should be continuous. In other words, you should always be planning, always looking ahead.

You should consider all possibilities that exist and consider exploiting as many of them as you can. At the same time, you should consider all of your available assets. Never dismiss anything or take anything for granted.

Effective planning means you should use the lowest level of support possible to carry out your mission. For a platoon leader, it means calling a firing battery—with six or eight cannons—for help rather than the entire artillery brigade. For a department manager, it means using the advice and assistance of people within the department or perhaps one level higher, rather than calling corporate headquarters with your problems or requests for assistance. If there is too much of a gap between the requester and the requestee, there is a greater chance that the request will get brushed aside, blown out of proportion, or lost in translation some other way.

Good predicting and planning means depending on sources of information that have been useful in the past and avoiding

Making sound predictions and plans includes allowing for flexibility.

unnecessary duplication of planning or information resources. It means occasionally looking outside the expected realm of possibility. Sometimes the best forecasting and preparation are due to thinking in ways not considered normal or typical.

Making sound predictions and plans includes allowing for flexibility. Hedge your bets and don't plan yourself into a corner. Just as with orienteering, you should always allow for the possibility of mid-course corrections.

Finally, sound predicting and planning calls for examining ways to protect your organization and your assets. When making calculations, you always need to consider means for guarding the gains you've already made.

While attending the U.S. Army Field Artillery School at Fort Sill, Oklahoma, I was handed an anonymous essay entitled

Baptism to Command. The author suggests that accurate fore-casting is not an inherent gift or a mystical sixth sense. "I say this [mythical gift of foresight] is hogwash created by fiction writers who know nothing of war," the author argues, suggest-ing that prediction is much more methodical and deliberative than instinctive.

> The great leaders that I have been privileged to observe in battle had one thing in common—deliberateness. The ability to think out the problem calmly. Weighing the pros and cons and arriving at sound solutions.

In business, making competent marketing predictions can certainly be less than mystical. Training and quality vice presi-dent Alan Fazzari maintains that strategic business plans should include practiced methods for making solid predictions. "For example, listening to the voice of the customer is the best way of indicating what the market—as well as our competi-tors—is going to do next." Fazzari suggests that focusing on short-term and long-term customer needs and wants and how to satisfy them makes for strong business forecasting.

But Fazzari warns not to feel obligated to stay on the path set by a forecast. "Let's face it. Markets today change on a dime—if not on a penny. Marketing plans should be dynamic and fluid. There really should be no beginning or end to any business projection."

No one expects one hundred percent accuracy in this fore-telling or its resulting strategies. But having a method for mak-ing levelheaded predictions strengthens the status of the team leader and helps maintain a solid foundation for all decision-making.

FOR CONSIDERATION:

- What is the difference between guessing the future and calculating what the future will bring?

- Have you ever had someone on your team or in your organization with an uncanny gift for making solid predictions? Looking back, was there something of a method to this person's gift?

- What are some forecasting techniques that have worked well for you in your area of expertise?

West Pointers Know the Enemy

You can't defeat the competition until you know who the competition is and what they're doing. From Sun Tzu to Norman Schwarzkopf, the great military minds throughout the history of warfare have agreed on the merits of learning as much as you can about your enemies before challenging them.

West Pointers are taught to base all operations on their reconnaissance of the enemy and the enemy's surroundings. Conducting recon is an integral part of the leader's planning process and has the potential to change how a mission is approached, or even change the mission itself. The information gathered during recon is essential to understanding one's enemies and knowing how to best move toward them and defeat them.

Reconnaissance of enemies includes determining how big they are, where they're located, what they're up to, how they're organized, and whether they're strong, experienced, or motivated. The ultimate aim is to predict what they're going to do next and where they're going to do it. That "what" and "where" influences the "how" of your attack.

Looking outside the scope of combat, any leadership challenge includes an "enemy" of sorts. The antagonist that a leader studies does not have to be a group of people in an overtly competitive setting. Researching and understanding any challenge or obstacle from the viewpoint of an adversary creates the proper state of mind for overcoming it and taking control. In his inspiring book, *Enduring Patagonia*, Gregory Crouch—a former Army Ranger and West Point classmate of mine—talks about facing the highest mountains of the earth as if they were enemies to be conquered. Appropriately, he conducts years of study before taking them on. In an early chapter, Crouch gets to know his upcoming "enemies"—the torturous, windswept mountains of Patagonia in Argentina and Chile—by exploring a similar setting:

> I got over a major obstacle when I climbed Yosemite's El Capitan. I had been told that any aspirant to the great mountain ranges of the world needed to be comfortable on the big walls of Yosemite. Able I proved to be; comfortable I was not. Two days into the El Cap climb, we had 2,000 feet below us and the wall soared over our heads like a granite ocean. I couldn't even sense the top of the route a thousand feet above us. I was lost in a sea of vertical granite and awash in fear. Terrified, I dry-heaved off the edge of the ledge where we spent the night. My technical skills were good enough, but mentally I barely held it together, and for Patagonia I would need to be comfortable on walls of this magnitude.

Crouch eventually understood enough about those mountains to go on seven expeditions to Patagonia. The highlight of his journeys was being a part of the first winter ascent of Cerro Torre's West Face.

Clearly, the correct time for Crouch to learn about his enemies occurred before engaging them. Had he only learned about these granite monsters in Patagonia at the start of the first expedition, the result would have been certain failure—perhaps death.

West Pointer Jack Amberg, a public affairs officer working for the U.S. Army in Japan, suggests that knowing the enemy is akin to understanding a problem before seeking a solution. "Mission or enemy analysis is not always done well," he says. "Lots of failed managers implement solutions without ever really knowing what the issue or challenge or mission really is.

The good leaders conduct thorough mission and enemy analyses and implement plans that relate to them. In other words, poor leaders concentrate on the solution—great leaders concentrate on understanding the problem."

In business, "enemy" often takes on a much more literal definition. It is the competition a company has to contend with when submitting bids and seeking customers. Commercial contract salesman Alan Shephard says becoming familiar with the competition is crucial. "You need to know who's entering the field and who's already in the field. You have to recognize how they bid and what they're going to put emphasis on in their proposals. Through competing bids, you need to learn about their size and their capabilities. Finally, you need to be on the lookout for enemies of the future—the small, almost inconsequential competitor whose business is ready to take off. *That's* the one who's going to sneak off one day with lots of the business."

> *Poor leaders concentrate on the solution—great leaders concentrate on understanding the problem.*

In commerce, there's an extra way to study and learn about one's potential enemy—you can join them! For example, if you aspire to someday own and operate the best hotel in your town, then the first step is to get hired by and work for a reputable hotel, learning and absorbing as much as you can along the way. Hey, it's not corporate espionage if you're loyal to the company while you're there, if you consistently put in an honest day's work, and if gathering information for your future makes you a good employee in the present. And if you find yourself challenging that same hotel in the future as the owner/operator of a rival inn, chances are they'll take pride in being kept on their toes competitively by someone they knew "way back when."

Charging forward against an unknown enemy is folly. The victorious leader has the enemy explored and figured out before the first day of combat begins.

FOR CONSIDERATION:

- When was the last time you got caught off guard by an "enemy" you should have known more about? What happened?

- Why might it be appropriate to base nearly all of your team's actions on those of your enemy?

- What is to be gained from knowing as much as you can about your enemies or obstacles?

The West Pointer Works Best at Three in the Morning

At West Point, cadets are taught to move by cover of the night. The soldiers of a combat patrolling unit not only keep themselves concealed by traveling in darkness, but they also ensure that the odds of being spotted during their trek are drastically reduced. Cadets are taught to adapt to the darkness and to embrace it, rather than fearing it. They're taught to identify people and objects by their nighttime silhouettes. They learn to rely on smells and sounds. They train in passing signals by whistling or tapping rocks. They practice walking quietly.

If the purpose of a nighttime patrol is to engage and destroy the enemy, then reaching a destination before the light of morning makes tactical sense as well. Night operation lessons are clear-cut enough: if you're on the go while others are resting, then you're going to go a long way, with few obstacles, and surprise a lot of people when they finally wake up.

Benjamin Franklin put forth a similar viewpoint when he said that the healthiest, wealthiest, and wisest people were those who went to sleep early so that they could be up and working before everyone else.

The notion that one can be productive during the quiet of the night is not lost on cadets at West Point. The Academy has changed its "lights out" policies back and forth throughout the years. During my last year as a cadet, the Corps was forced to turn out the lights at 11:30 PM and go to bed. This policy prompted the Honor Committee to debate at length whether covering the windows with a thick blanket to conceal a study light from the Officer of the Guard was, in essence, making a dishonorable statement or simply carrying out mischief aimed at extending a night of study. During my other three cadet years, when "lights out" was not mandatory, I made a habit of finding the quietest, most private spot in the old stacks of the library. I would use that solitude to study, write, plan projects, and strategize the remainder of my academic plan. The next day, I would make up the sleep during free time between classes and, depending on how dark the lecture halls were, during the more boring academic addresses. The weekend, too, served as a time of battery recharging after a week of working while others slept. I finished my time at the Academy ranked academically almost exactly at the midpoint of my class—not bad considering I was competing against a very smart group of people, many of whom had been valedictorians and salutatorians of their high school classes. I'm convinced to this day that my ranking had everything to do with thinking, planning, and working while others were sleeping.

Keep in mind that the notion of "doing while others are dreaming" can work well figuratively as well as literally. Living with this mindset means discovering and capturing positions of advantage before others even know they exist. It means researching and pondering what the "next big thing" will be and staking a claim on it. It means moving fast and gaining the lead. Jason Jennings and Laurence Haughton write about such a business philosophy in their book *It's Not the Big that Eat the Small...It's the Fast that Eat the Slow*. They suggest that the flourishing team leader is one who antici-

> *When others are "asleep," the smart, innovative leader has his team on the move.*

pates trends, spots business developments, and then makes fast decisions to take advantage of them. They explain that someone can spot fruitful, profit-generating trends by surfing the Web, scrutinizing what's on television, and studying one's physical surroundings. The key is to study a move and conduct it cautiously, but also to complete it deliberately and promptly and, to keep others guessing, to carry it out quietly—"at night," so to speak.

Technical service manager Larry Nykwest agrees. "I've worked for the biggest paper company in the world and one of the smallest," he says, "and the way big companies or small companies win the battle for customers is quick response time." Nykwest says that by offering customers a team of rapid, service-oriented technical people, companies can take business away from competitors who are "asleep" or complacent. "I once visited customers in Michigan, Pennsylvania, and New York in just a few days," he says, "replying in person as quickly as I could to customer comments and concerns." Nykwest adds proudly that he often gets calls from the customers of *other* paper companies who have heard about him, asking for technical advice. "If they're calling me for help instead of my competition, I know I'm eventually going to get that business."

When others are "asleep," the smart, innovative leader has his team on the move. By the time the competition wakes up, the leader's team will already have made its strategic move and left the area, setting out for the next competitive challenge.

FOR CONSIDERATION:

- What is to be gained from getting up extremely early in the morning and planning or working before others are awake?

- What does the phrase "doing while others are dreaming" mean to you?

- What are some ways to sense an advantageous move before anyone else?

- What has worked for you in the past?

The West Pointer Tactically Concentrates the Attack

If you push against a cement wall with your hand, chances are you'll see very little result for your effort. But if you take an ice pick and push it against that same wall with the same amount of force, you might see a mark or a small hole. If you find a soft spot in the concrete and push hard enough, you just might bore right through. The difference has to do with finding the weakness and converging the force. That's what tactically concentrating the attack is all about when facing an enemy or a challenge.

The process of concentrating your force begins with gathering information. For the combat platoon leader, it means going on patrols. The recon patrol is meant essentially to study the enemy from a distance, collecting as much useful data as possible. The purpose of the infiltrating patrol is to pass undetected if possible through enemy boundaries to get a close-up picture of what the enemy looks like and is doing. The probing patrol is meant to quietly harass the enemy just enough to draw fire, exposing enemy firing positions and revealing gaps or weak spots in his defenses. Once these defensive vulnerabilities are uncovered, the platoon leader determines how to exploit them. Driving the most force possible through these avenues of enemy susceptibility is a channeling of resources for the most dramatic effect.

For the successful business manager, the tactics are really no different. When we examine the inspiring success stories of our day, we don't necessarily admire the businessperson who conquers everything in all ways. More likely, we marvel over the keen entrepreneur who becomes immersed in a market segment, studies the needs of consumers, and sees the gaps left by suppliers. And then, focusing lots of time, energy, effort, and imagination on those gaps, this innovator creates a product or a service that takes hold and grows rapidly. We gape in wonder at the person who bores through concrete with an ice pick.

A terrific business example of concentrating the attack is the Portland-based Leatherman Tool Group. Much to the surprise of many, the company's name does not allude to a trade or to the rugged nature of the person who carries the popular Leatherman tool. The company is named after its founder and president, Tim Leatherman, an English teacher, mechanical engineer, and world traveler who started the company over a quarter of a century ago. As early as the late 1960s, Leatherman spotted a gap in the personal tool market: there were no pliers with knives.

Creating prototypes out of cardboard in 1975, Leatherman focused eight years of effort and energy into producing a marketable tool—a set of pliers with knives and screwdrivers that folded into the handles. Starting out by offering his innovative utensil through a few camping catalogues, Tim Leatherman found that he could barely keep up with the orders. All these years later, Leatherman Tool Group employs 450 people in Oregon and

The effective leader knows the fights that are worth fighting and directs all effort and energy toward them.

manufactures two million Leatherman tools a year. Without a doubt, Leatherman saw a gap in the market—a weakness in his "enemy's" defenses, if you will—and tactically concentrated everything he had on that one area. His victory is legendary.

It should be mentioned that knowing where to concentrate your resources might mean looking at the bigger picture. Along with recognizing where to converge your power in one battle against one enemy, you might also need to identify *which* battles to select and even *which* enemies you want to take on. The effective leader knows the fights that are worth fighting and directs all effort and energy toward them. Spreading oneself out too thinly—or even just too evenly—can mean many half-fought battles. It's an old saying, but "choose your battles wisely" is worth repeating.

The good team leader understands that sweat, drudgery, and anguish do not necessarily equal victory over the competition. Concentrating that exertion, however, on the points where the impact will be felt the most makes the conquest more likely.

FOR CONSIDERATION:

- Where should you be concentrating your team's efforts right now?

- How tactically could you be converging your resources toward a gap or weak spot in a competitor's "defenses"?

- What priorities are worth a concentration of your time and energy? What "enemies" might be preoccupying you or taking up too much of your time and energy?

West Pointers Don't Attack the Enemy—
They Attack *Through* the Enemy

West Pointers are taught that, in combat, making contact with the enemy is only the first step. The platoon leader knows that the successful mission doesn't mean attacking the enemy, but pushing to the farthest area of the enemy's location. The platoon achieves this total victory by shocking and confusing the enemy, exploiting the enemy's gaps and weak points, and by forcing its way decisively across enemy territory.

Unless the mission is to harass the enemy and retreat, or to probe for weak points or conduct some other type of reconnaissance, as a platoon leader your goal is to surprise, overwhelm, and destroy the enemy and then to consolidate all the elements of your team at the rear of the enemy's camp. In other words, your goal isn't to attack the enemy, but rather to attack *through* the enemy.

When applying this intense, graphic outlook to noncombat ambitions, keep in mind that even if you don't consider the more mundane competitive situations of your life in this light, your rivals surely do. Football coaching legend Vince Lombardi made the point that all types of competition are similar and must be tackled the same way. "Running a football team is no different than running any other kind of organization—an army, a political party, or a business," he said. "The principles are the same. The object is to win—to beat the other guy. Maybe that sounds hard or cruel. I don't think it is."

The quintessential business example of seizing the opportunity and overtaking the competition is Wal-Mart. For years, I have taught economics to undergraduate and graduate school students, and every semester I mention how much I admire the Sam Walton story, especially how it demonstrates taking the competition by surprise and continuing to confound and defeat them completely. Wal-Mart is the world's largest retailer with over $200 billion in annual sales, over three thousand stores in the United States, and over one thousand stores elsewhere in the world. Unlike several discount retailers, Wal-Mart does not have a history that extends back to the turn of the twentieth century: the first Wal-Mart store opened in the United States in 1962. As recently as twenty-five years ago, company sales had not yet passed $1 billion. But with a sound business plan and subsequent diversification into grocery stores and membership warehouses, the company went on to solidly dominate much of the retail marketplace.

Microeconomics teaches the concept of "economies of scale." Put simply, the bigger a company becomes, the more it produces, orders, or sells, and the lower its long-run average cost grows. The reason: ordering in bulk is cheaper, even for companies. Traditional United States retailers understood and utilized this model throughout the 1900s. But respecting the restrictions of economies of scale—particularly that it requires lots of retail customers—they only set up stores in highly pop-ulated areas, and stayed away from midsized or smaller cities and towns. Sam Walton saw their hesitation to enter these mar-kets and "exploited the enemy's gap," so to speak. Sensing that these relatively smaller localities would be attracted to the lower prices of a big discount retailer, he set about building Wal-Mart stores in these communities.

Once the other retail giants realized what was going on, in many cases, it was too late. Many of these towns could support one large discount store, but not two or more. By taking a chance on these smaller municipalities and beating other dis-counters to them, Sam Walton clearly overtook and over-whelmed the competition. As the company's long-run average cost continued to drop, his stores began vying for and winning business in larger markets as well. He also went on to revolutionize the way products were bought by ordering supplies as they were needed in a highly responsive, streamlined inventory system. Again, the Wal-Mart story is an admirable example of taking on and beating formidable competition.

Management academic director Esther Taitsman suggests that your enemy's weak points might be its gaps in market strategy or

Focus marketing efforts on those areas where you dominate.

product appeal. If there are market needs that even a strong competitor is overlooking, you might be able to stage a successful attack. "When we assess Thomas Edison State College's competition for prospective students, we invariably wind up focusing our marketing efforts on those areas—such as student customer service or academic flexibility—where we feel we dominate." Having taught at the college over the last few years and watching their numbers grow, I suspect their tactics are successful.

Remember, your attack doesn't stop when you reach the enemy camp. You attack *through* the camp and regroup to the rear of the site. A sound, competitive business strategy should work the same way.

FOR CONSIDERATION:

- In business, what is to be gained by taking an aggressive stance toward the competition?

- How do the notions of surprise and conquest relate to your business?

- In your area of business, how might you gain the upper hand in taking over a market?

The West Pointer Is Always Thinking about the Next Mission

Over the years, "lighting up plebes" (yelling at them for the sport of it) has largely become obsolete at the Academy as a rite of passage. But, honestly, I found it entirely appropriate for the senior cadets, the firsties, to turn up the heat every now and then and see what the Company D-4 fourth-class cadets—our Duke plebes—were made of. We weren't the toughest company in the Corps for running out fourth-class cadets, but things could get pretty hot in Dukedom when the firsties wanted it to be.

Once, after a rather pleasant night of plebe smoking, I sat with a few other firsties in the company lounge and discussed who had shown some mettle and who hadn't. The plebes would never hear about it, but we generally approved of the way they had withstood the intensity of the grilling and the amount of cadet trivia—"fourth-class knowledge"—they had displayed.

An off-the-wall topic came up: what did we think about while yelling at plebes? Did we concentrate on our "smoking" technique? Did we gauge the responses of the plebes? Did we think about the next knowledge question to ask?

Pat Matthews, a passionate classmate of mine who lived for all things military (and still does), made an attention-grabbing observation. "I think about the dinner menu." The room went silent: he had thrown us a curve. Matthews continued. "Sure. I think about what I've read on the posted menu for dinner, if I'm going to like it, skip it, or lean heavily on the salad. Hell, if it wasn't for lighting up plebes, I'd never have time to think about anything."

We all laughed knowingly. Pat was right: the last thing anyone ever really thought about while shouting down fourth-class cadets was the event itself. Once an upperclass cadet became good at bellowing, he could put himself on automatic pilot and think about all sorts of things while the disciplining was going on. The funny thing is, it also worked the other way. Toward the end of plebe year, a fourth-class cadet could stand there and get smoked while *he* was contemplating the later events of the day. At any given time, a cadet was thinking about the next phase of the game—even while administering or enduring a plebe grilling.

I would guess that this forward-thinking mindset stays with the West Pointer. The good officer instinctively considers "what's on the menu" while other things—the extraordinary things—are going on around him. Sure, a manager has to "Be Here Now," that superb principle about not being preoccupied that I learned when I first was hired by Bell Atlantic (now Verizon). However, a good manager doesn't become obsessed with the present. The effective leader is always thinking about the future, about enemies that aren't enemies yet and missions that haven't yet been assigned. The effective leader can predict the battles that are far from being fought, but merit speculation and planning.

> *The effective leader is always thinking about the future.*

One of my textbooks as a cadet was *Definitions and Doctrine of the Military Art* by John I. Alger. Alger concludes the book by discussing what practitioners of the military art need to look for in the future. He could just as easily be writing about the global marketplace instead of the global battlefield, particularly when he discusses technology, preparedness, professionalism, and logistics. Large sections of his prose could easily be inserted into any business book. A case in point:

The future belongs to those who dare. And daring requires courage born of loyalty and wisdom born of experience. Courage and wisdom cannot be acquired from books or professors—no matter how brilliant and erudite they might be. Loyalty and experience, however, can be acquired through understanding and education, and history can provide countless examples that contribute to the further appreciation of both.... [T]he more we learn, the more we come to recognize our own ignorance. For some, the circle of knowledge evokes pessimism; for others, the circle of knowledge gives encouragement, because each time the frontier of darkness is pushed back, we improve the quality of our lives and the lives of others.

That's why the West Pointer is always thinking about the next mission. With another mission comes another potential victory, as well as another step toward achieving an improvement for the team and for the organization.

Commercial contract salesman Alan Shephard says it best. "If you're not thinking about the next project, the next goal, then you're starving. In December, I've planned backwards three months from what I hope to be doing in March. That three-month timeline is my lifeline."

FOR CONSIDERATION:

- Do you know someone who's always thinking ahead? Why does such a person command respect and admiration?

- Why might it be a good idea to always be focused on the next mission?

- What does the next mission hold for your team? Your organization?

CHAPTER EIGHT

PROFICIENCY

BE THE EXPERT
AND SHARE THE KNOWLEDGE

The West Pointer Is Constantly Seeking Self-Improvement

The first West Point Principle of Leadership is "Know yourself and seek self-improvement." To the West Pointer, complacency is the same as stagnation. The West Pointer is never content, never still, as the West Point manner dictates that managers really *can't* settle, even if they want to. The viewpoint is that, at any given time, a manager is either improving or depreciating, but never set.

West Point graduate Bob Doran is the production manager for Herff Jones, Inc., a manufacturer and distributor of corporate and college memorabilia items such as rings, certificates, and awards. Doran works at the company's fine papers plant in Scranton, Pennsylvania, a facility that makes diplomas, diploma covers, and graduation announcements. Besides supervising people, Doran's job includes monitoring workflow and scrutinizing different efficiency indicators.

Doran suggests that continuous change is important in order for a manager to thrive and be successful. "If I sit still for even a minute, I'm failing," he says. "I try to finish every day knowing a little bit more about my trade or finding out something new by trying something a little different."

He says that, if nothing else, the accelerated pace of today's technology requires that managers push themselves to change and improve. He uses his own occupation as an example. "The printing industry depends on the skills of people as connected to the machinery they have. All the time, the way that we print tends to change because of some new technical or chemical advancement. As a manager, I have to be up on those advancements, their pluses and minuses investment-wise, and the skill requirements related to these advancements. If I'm doing my job right, I'm the *first* to know and understand these things." He also suggests that these improvements are not always apparent. "If you're going to improve yourself and your team, you have to be open to any suggestion. Sometimes, the best idea initially seems the most off-the-wall."

Doran is an active duty Army Reserve major who has trained extensively as a civil affairs advisor. I asked him what sort of global assignments he might have coming up. "If I told you, I'd have to kill you," he quipped. He notes that his ongoing military experiences often render his civilian management decisions easier to make. "As a manager, I always feel of clear mind when returning from Reserve duty," he says. "The decisions back at the plant become almost obvious. I just choose to do the right things for the team and for the mission."

Such "right things" include constantly seeking self-improvement. "The great managers I've worked for have set personal goals for themselves, not just focused on their individual accomplishments, but on how they can relate to the big picture," Doran remarks. "Seeking self-improvement means a never-ending drive toward becoming one with that big picture, to comprehending the smallest things about the largest issues."

Doran believes that such a personal outlook on self-discovery lends itself well to creating a vision for, motivating, training, and leading a team. "The Army consistently trains its people using the same

A pioneering manager is a dynamic manager, always learning, always improving, and always open to change.

format—introducing the task, teaching the conditions, and declaring the standards for success," he says. "That's how a leader needs to implement self-improvement, and that's how a leader needs to train the team. New task. New conditions. New standards. Over and over again."

Doran says he feels no greater sense of accomplishment than when he discovers a method of self-improvement, learns it, perfects it, and then relates it in some fashion to his team. "Accomplishing team goals by starting first with self-improvement is the ultimate good feeling of achievement," he says.

Senior design engineer Chuck Granitz agrees. "Constantly learning, constantly trying new things—that's important." After forty years in the business of making aircraft engines, he says he is still learning. "I want to strive for new ways of doing things and to share them. There are always ways to make better engines— engines with greater thrust-to-weight ratios, more efficiency, less noise, less pollution and maintenance. The improvement process must start on a personal level and be ongoing."

A pioneering manager is a dynamic manager, always learning, always improving, and always open to change.

FOR CONSIDERATION:

- Do you agree with the view that, as a manager, you can never "settle in," that you're either getting better or getting worse as a leader at any given moment?

- What have you done in the past to seek self-improvement? What might you do in the future?

- What personal strategy might you put together to better relate yourself to the big picture for your team and your organization?

- How do you think seeking self-improvement might convert into seeking and achieving team improvement?

The West Pointer is "Technically and Tactically Proficient"

The second West Point Principle of Leadership is "Be technically and tactically proficient." The statement seems obvious enough: a manager should know the practical and procedural aspects of his team's job, and he should be deliberate and discerning when planning itineraries for his team. However, the significance of this principle is that it appropriately fights the old stereotype of the boss who is behind his entire team and who manages in a technical field he knows nothing about. The technically and tactically proficient leader is no empty suit. He knows enough about the complexities of his profession to keep his team well-trained and well-practiced, and he knows enough about ongoing developments in his field to keep the team pointed in the right direction.

For a military unit or a business firm, there's something of a management dilemma that is ongoing and unlikely to ever be resolved. The organization can pull its leaders from within, such as selecting "officer material" from the enlisted ranks or choosing production-line workers to attend management training. Alternatively, the organization can draw fresh talent and outside knowledge by hiring from external sources, such as recruiting West Point cadets from high schools or hiring managers directly from business schools. The drawback to always hiring from within is that management can become stale or too inbred. The drawback to always hiring from outside sources is that the "smart boss who knows nothing" might end up being more than just a stereotype.

The solution probably includes an appropriate mix of recruiting from both sources. Hiring some leaders from within allows the organization to screen its future managers up close, even for years, and to keep invested technical experience in the house. There's also a pretty strong argument that people hold a degree of respect for bosses who work their way up through the ranks. On the other hand, hiring from outside the organization allows the company to pull young, energetic talent into the house and mold it accordingly, as well as seeking great minds from competing corporations. It provides the company with an appropriate level of management objectivity, as leaders begin their assignments unhampered by internal prejudgments. Finally, the externally hired leader shows up with a clean slate, free from the personal baggage that might come with being hired from within.

However, for the leader starting fresh in an organization, getting up-to-speed technically and tactically should be an urgent priority. And staying proficient should always be an imperative part of managing the team.

> *Staying proficient should always be an imperative part of managing the team.*

Pat McHenry is a West Point graduate and a regional assistant sales manager. He suggests that a great leader is a technically sound leader. "In most aspects of my job, I try to be just as well-versed as anyone on my team," he says. "In the Army, I was never as good on the machine gun as the enlisted specialist who knew that weapon inside and out. But I knew how to take it apart, clean it, put it back together, zero it, and fire it. And—in a pinch—I could have manned that weapon against an enemy. The same goes for my current job. I have to feel comfortable that, at any given time, I could fill in for anyone on my team."

McHenry's philosophy applies to the tactical aspect of his job as well. As a former Army Ranger, he has carried much of his "hoo-ahh" motivation into business sales. When talking about sales, he speaks in terms of strategies, tactics, and targeting customer markets. "I try to know at any given time where the new business opportunities are and direct the team to those areas."

Marketing manager Lisa Tawney Scheuerman finds leadership strength in her technical know-how. "I can get on that phone and sell as well as anyone on my team, and occasionally I'll show them. Leading by example gains a lot of respect, which means I'm able to ask a lot of my team."

A manager shouldn't be just a figurehead. The good leader knows and appreciates the technical aspects of each job on the team and knows how to guide the team tactically through the challenges that lie ahead.

FOR CONSIDERATION:

- Have you ever had a boss who knew as much, if not more, about your job than you did?

- What impression did that boss leave on you and the team?

- What are some of the technical aspects of the job positions on your team? How proficient are you in those aspects?

- What are some of the tactical aspects of your profession? Where is your team headed within that field?

- What are you doing to help point your team in the right direction?

- How might you concentrate on the smaller, practical aspects of your team members' duties while staying focused on the big picture at the same time?

West Pointers Share What They Learn

When I was an enlisted soldier with the United States Field Artillery at Fort Hood, Texas, our six-gun cannon battery spent a lot of training time "in the field." That's the way the artillery functioned. If you weren't in the field, you were either prepping your gear to go into the field or cleaning it after coming out of the field. It was stressful, tiring, muddy work. But when things came together and we started sending rounds "downrange," all the drudgery seemed worth it. Watching and listening to the muzzle blasts of those firing cannons was probably the most motivating thing I did as a soldier and later as an officer. As I mentioned above, hurling cannon rounds into the air onto targets as far as thirty miles away gives one a serious sense of authority.

As a fire direction specialist, one of my most important peacetime jobs was calculating the firing safety data for our training locations. Specifically, our team had to determine the left and right limits to where the cannons could point, and compute the limits for how close and how far out the crews could send rounds. Firing beyond those limits meant potentially lethal rounds landing somewhere outside the impact training area. As you might imagine, computing safety data and delivering it to the cannon crews was a task everyone took seriously.

I remember my battery commander, Captain Robert Sprague—a West Point graduate who inspired me to apply for admission to the Academy—poking his head into the fire direction center. "Is the safety data finished?" he asked.

"Yes, sir. We're just about ready to send it to the gun line."

"Don't do that," he ordered. "Call the youngest soldier from each gun section up here and show him how to compute the safety data for his howitzer. Don't overwhelm him; don't let him write his own data down. When he leaves, hand him the data you computed. But when he leaves, I want him to understand a little about how this team figures those limits."

"Yes, sir."

And so, instead of sending rounds downrange as quickly as possible—usually the mark of a squared-away firing unit—we spent about two hours training the greenest soldiers in our battery on how to compute safety data. We didn't show them too much, and—as Captain Sprague had ordered—we didn't let them write down their computations out of concern that the uncertain information would make its way to the gun line. But when each soldier left our tent, I believe he had a better understanding of how safety data was extracted and computed from a map and where those numbers came from. And, more importantly, by looking at that map, each soldier understood that those cannon rounds didn't disappear into thin air once they were fired. They landed somewhere *on that map*, and if it was the wrong place, someone could get hurt. By sharing what we knew, we were making the firing unit a safer group of soldiers.

The good leader understands the synergy of shared information.

The good leader understands the synergy of shared information. Put simply, when a manager shares facts, figures, and experiences, they interact with the wisdom and skills of the people on the team, resulting in a combination of knowledge that's greater than the initial fragments of data.

Sharing information runs contrary to the behaviors of stereotypical bosses who squirrel away knowledge. In an effort to underscore their authority, and perhaps their "irreplaceability," these managers feel the need to keep what they know to themselves. They are not so much tightfisted as they are afraid—unwilling to pass along their experience for fear that it will bring them down to the level of their team members. Little do they realize that the pedestal on which they imagine themselves is shaky at best and often nonexistent in the eyes of the people they supervise. Rather than look up to the smart boss who is stingy with information, team members tend to revere the manager who wants to share the wealth.

Engineer and building operations manager Tom Glynn claims that sharing information with your team displays leadership strength. "Sharing what you know means letting your team know you're not weak, that you don't feel threatened by other people having access to what's going on." Furthermore, Glynn says, people will reciprocate the courtesy of being informed. "The more you info you share, the more info you gain."

Glynn also suggests that sharing information means learning about team members' individual strengths. "If I tell them what I know," he says, "I can recognize their competencies through their responses."

An effective leader never hoards information with the hope of using it as a power wedge. The good leader is an open book of wisdom and past experiences, understanding the synergy of sharing and appreciating the motivational influence of keeping others knowledgeable.

FOR CONSIDERATION:

- Have you recently had a good experience sharing professional knowledge with someone on your team? What happened?

- What about relating past experiences—"war stories," so to speak? Have you told one recently to positive effect? Do you see a result?

- What is to be gained by sharing learned knowledge and past experiences with the members of your team?

The West Pointer Keeps Everyone Informed

Just as the team leader should share technical know-how and learned information with the team, so should the leader keep everyone informed about events and plans within the organization.

I have worked for organizations that kept nearly everything secret—business strategies, marketing plans, schedules, etc. Admittedly, some of it was outside the scope of my team, and we didn't need to preoccupy ourselves with it. But a huge portion of what was kept under wraps need not have been. Whatever benefit was gained by keeping secrets was more than offset by feelings of detachment, isolation, and needless anxiety. Team members often believed that if there was something to hide, it couldn't be good for the people who weren't privy to it. The assessment was almost always wrong, but the mindset was nearly as damaging to the team as the wrongfully conjectured circumstances.

People inherently crave information and yearn to be kept informed. The best supervisors I have ever worked for—in the military and in business—played to that innate desire. They are the bosses who came around to each workstation, explaining one-on-one how each of our assignments was going to fit into the team plan and the organizational puzzle. They are the bosses who released large batches of reports rather than trickling information over time. This open management seems rare, and that's a shame. People profoundly appreciate the leader who keeps everyone informed.

Contrast the open manager with the one who conceals big-picture information as some sort of device for power control. Just as with technical know-how, hoarding strategic information gives some bosses a false sense of security, an "I-have-something-you-don't" attitude toward team members. Most people recognize the game and, in my experience, only a few willingly play along. Handing out information in piecemeal fashion is an unfortunate sign of managerial insecurity.

As well as creating an appropriate atmosphere of openness and mission belongingness, keeping everyone informed has another benefit: it generates feedback. As mentioned above, the best advice often comes from the places you least expect it. By updating your team members on the bigger missions, you're likely to get suggestions that will keep the team on track and, perhaps, even alter these bigger missions in a constructive way.

Keep in mind that it's not necessary for everyone on the team to be aware of everyone else's activities constantly; nor is it necessary for everyone to be tuned in at all times to a large picture that's three or four levels above the team's mission. Consider the notion of "organizational channeling," where people's individual talents and energy are channeled into the individual tasks at hand, instead of having large groups of people in conference rooms forever getting filled in on grand company tactics.

> *People profoundly appreciate the leader who keeps everyone informed.*

Military groups work largely on a need-to-know basis, mostly for reasons of confidentiality. Considering the fast pace of today's marketplace and taking into account how quickly corporate espionage by a competitor can foil a long-range business plan, it seems reasonable that some strategizing remain at the level where it was formulated.

However, to the extent that people perform better when they feel they own a part of the big picture, keeping them informed pays big dividends in motivation and personal responsibility. And, again, when people know what's going on, they can lend their own advice, which is often invaluable.

Supply and production manager Rich Vincz says, "Keep the information as straightforward as you can. Portray the big goals as simply as possible. If you think they're attainable, let people know it. Listen to the reactions of your team and take note of what suggestions they make."

The caring leader ensures that everyone on the team knows the goals of the team, why these goals are important, and what the team is doing to reach them.

FOR CONSIDERATION:

- Have you ever had a boss who made it a point to keep everyone on the team informed and updated? How did you feel about that boss?

- Why do you suppose most people appreciate being kept "in the loop"?

- What are the benefits to keeping people abreast of upcoming team priorities and changes? How do people profit from knowing the organization's big picture?

- What are the limits to passing along information to the team? Are there times when some secrecy is required? Are there times when it's important to keep the team focused on the smaller picture?

- What is to be gained from everybody knowing and understanding their team's goals?

The West Pointer Reads

When I tell people that my first semester in college was a twenty-credit-hour semester, they generally think I'm exaggerating or mistaken. But that was, indeed, my first semester at the United States Military Academy. It's a brutal stretch that produces many academic casualties. From calculus to chemistry to English composition to United States military history to general psychology to the military profession and military instruction, it is a rigorous system of learning that cadets affectionately refer to as *the fire-hose method*. That is, learning at West Point is much like being thirsty and having a fire hose turned on in your face. Sure you get your thirst quenched, but you also get pounded in the process. The expression also suggests that lots of the water—or information—sadly gets lost in the deluge (except by the geniuses, of which there are some).

The reading assignments for those academic subjects are extensive and abundant. On top of them is a regimen of cadet requirements that doesn't lend itself well to academic study. The Academy almost jokingly suggests that cadets should put two hours of preparation into each hour of classroom time. In other words, two hours of homework per one hour in class. On certain days, you would need a twenty-seven-hour day with no sleep to mathematically accommodate that requirement. And while the semester course loads eventually taper off a bit and you get used to strategizing what's important to look at and what can be skimmed, the reading obligations continue throughout your stay like a fast-moving river with a current that you can't swim against.

Like lots of things at West Point, however, the larger results of the process are more important and positive than the small oddities that never make sense. In the case of the academic load, the oddity is an academic schedule and reading requirements that most people are never able to meet. The larger result is a lifelong respect for time and task prioritization and, ironically, a wonderful appreciation for reading. The West Point graduate leaves the Academy with an insatiable appetite for books.

It's not easy to pinpoint when the transformation occurs—when the cadet goes from loathing books to being drawn to them. But I would argue that the desire to absorb as much of the written word as time allows has much to do with a West Pointer's inclination toward exercising winning leadership. Making good management choices starts with having lots of choices available. Lots of choices means lots of information, and lots of information means lots learned. And there *is* a lot to be learned from wading through an abundance of books on anything and everything.

> *Good managers always have books nearby.*

When casually asked, "Have you read any good books lately?" the effective leader often has a fresh list, including at least one book she's currently reading. Managers are frequently drawn to books on leadership, business, and time management, including books on motivating and influencing others. There also are some not-so-apparent sources of instruction, such as books on history for the manager who wants to learn from the experiences of others. And there are books that provide off-beat information, such as those on stress management and self-actualization. Finally, there are books that serve as sources of personal inspiration, such as those about heroes or people who have overcome adversity.

There's something to be said for reading as a means of mental workout. Books are beneficial to the manager not only for gathering knowledge but also for working out and keeping blood flowing to the mind. A good novel is an appropriate, relaxing diversion.

Good managers always have books nearby, and not just books on leadership, history, or business. Powerful knowledge comes from a variety of literary sources, and even just from the exercise of your mind through the workout of reading.

FOR CONSIDERATION:

- Have you read any good books lately?

- What is it about reading that might make great leaders out of good leaders?

- Have you ever read a book that provided you with some good, practical management lessons?

- Is there a book that you've used for personal and professional inspiration?

- Do you benefit from relaxation reading?

The West Pointer Has a Hobby

As a cadet, I was astonished by the number of clubs and activities at the Academy. With so many academic and military obligations, I figured no one would be interested in joining anything that took up the few precious unscheduled minutes we had available. I was wrong. Cadets signed up in droves for club athletic teams, such as rugby, water polo, and power lifting. There were marksmanship clubs for pistol, skeet, and trap. There were clubs for chess, fishing, and scuba diving. There were glee clubs, the gospel choir, the spirit band, and the cadets who ran the radio station WKDT. There were prayer groups and cultural groups. And—as if cadets didn't already have their fill of academic work—there were academic clubs, lots of them, including film, fine arts, history, debating, electronics, and engineering. In spite of feeling overwhelmed by a packed day of scheduled events at West Point, I followed suit and joined the spirit band and the class committee.

Looking back, it's not so difficult to understand why we gravitated toward these activities. We *needed* the distraction. Although the time-management purists might have warned against planning events during our scarce free time, we did so instinctively, knowing the hobbies would provide us with mental diversion, stimulation, and relaxation.

Sometimes it's vital to take the human mind away from the task at hand. There's unquestionably a diminishing point of return to what you get from your brain as you apply it over time to any task. The mind dulls, the task lags. Taking the occasional pleasant distraction gives your mind a break.

Having a hobby keeps the mind sharp. I would suggest that even the most apparently noncerebral hobby—like fitness running or fishing—allows us to take in life, strategize upcoming events, and contemplate the world at large. We return to the task with a refreshed outlook and a cleared mental readiness.

Along with keeping the mind sharp, a hobby also keeps the mind relaxed. "You have to de-stress," says Goodrich Chairman, President, and CEO Marshall Larsen. He likes to bird-hunt and has gotten involved with Scouting. "At Goodrich, we just about force people to take vacation," he says, pointing out the company's policy of not allowing large amounts of vacation time to carry over into future years. The point is to get people to unwind. Larsen also suggests that a manager's willingness to take vacation is a good indicator of how well he has prepared

Along with keeping the mind sharp, a hobby also keeps the mind relaxed.

the organization to run without him. "I just took two straight weeks," he boasts. "If I can't be gone for two weeks, then I haven't done a very good job."

As a team leader, you don't want to force people into certain hobbies or after-work activities—and you shouldn't take it personally if they don't share your passion for, say, running marathons or reading military literature. But you should set the example and encourage the overworked people on your team to step back, take some time out, and pursue some type of activity not related to work. It will keep them from burning out.

And if you do take up a hobby, make sure you do so because you find it enjoyable, and not because it's what others are doing or telling you to do. For example, if you really don't enjoy golfing but you do it because it's what you're coworkers are doing, there may be politically advantageous reasons for making that choice. But don't call it a hobby—what you're doing there is just more work. A stress-relieving, mind-soothing, and potentially thought-provoking hobby is one that you take on in a genuinely eager and enthusiastic way. It's a pleasure.

The West Pointer is not consumed by work. A good team leader understands the importance of mind diversion and encourages everyone to take life breathers.

FOR CONSIDERATION:

- Do you have a pastime that serves as a positive mental diversion?

- Do you have a hobby that keeps your mind sharp?

- Do you have a hobby that keeps your mind relaxed?

- How might you encourage an overworked team member to take the occasional breather and find a hobby?

CHAPTER NINE

LOYALTY

EXERCISE IT UP AND DOWN

The West Pointer Only Questions the Boss behind Closed Doors

As a West Point plebe, I was not so much afraid of a particular firstie as I was of the firstie *machine*. That is, as my classmates and I were pinging the hallways and carrying out our chores, the hounding and interrogating by the first-class cadets seemed more of a concerted effort, rather than a group of individuals each taking a swat. The firsties in my company all seemed to know what we had already been asked and what we didn't know, where we were coming from, where we were going, and they exploited our weaknesses and agendas to the fullest. They knew what buttons to push. They knew which plebes would break first and which plebes needed a little more work. And they all apparently understood the boundaries of behavior in handling the plebes—how far they could go in traumatizing us without going over the top (or at least not getting caught if they did).

The well-orchestrated nature of this aggravation suggested to me that it was being commanded and controlled by a tight cadet company leadership. I imagined them sitting in a room late at night, laughing, planning all the hoops they were going to make us jump through the next day. Or better yet, they were down at Benny's Lounge, sharing beers and conniving ways to make our lives miserable. They seemed like a tight bunch, and I imagined their camaraderie grew with each smoked plebe. What a wonderful pastime lighting us up must have been for these great friends.

Following my plebe year, I was surprised to find out that my company's cadet leadership was comprised of people who generally weren't great friends. They didn't hate each other, but apparently there had been large philosophical differences on how the company should be run and how the fourth-class system should be implemented. High up on the list of big disagreements was determining the nature, frequency, and intensity of plebe grilling. I

Leaders loyal to the message portray a cohesiveness that's positive and contagious.

was stunned to learn that there had been huge arguments over how to deal with the bunch of us. It was difficult for me to visualize these heated discussions, given how lock-step the discipline had been.

What made the coordinated effort so effective and convincing was that these disagreements had taken place behind closed doors. All my classmates and I saw was the same message over and over again: "Plebes, you'd better be straight, 'cause it's gonna get hot if you're not." Surely, had we known that there was dissention among the upperclass cadets on how we were to be treated, we would have slacked off intentionally, testing the system for weak spots. But since all we saw was uniformity in attitude, we didn't dare do anything but muscle through the intensity.

I learned a lot about leadership from that group of first-class cadets. For that matter, I learned a lot about followership as well. The solution to staff effectiveness seemed to be to keep the dissent and debate hidden. Once the meeting was concluded, the effective staff carried out the leader's decision earnestly and stayed "on message." As I continued my cadet journey, I tried to follow the philosophy of lively debate behind closed doors and total loyalty once the doors were opened.

Adhering to this leadership method has also translated well in the business world. Although I might strenuously disagree with a policy my boss is implementing, I always go forth into the organization arguing the boss's viewpoint. It is a "loyalty up" that managers appreciate.

Uniformity of message is not only good for the staff, it's good for the organization as well. Members of a company work best when they're given a clear direction. Open disagreements among a group's leaders cause confusion and often provoke unnecessary lines being drawn and sides being taken. The result is a corrosive work setting. By staying loyal to decisions once they're made, leaders portray a cohesiveness that's positive and contagious.

As mentioned earlier, the smart business leader allows for criticism and the questioning of decisions. But when the meeting is over and the door opens, the staff stays "on message" and becomes one voice. The good leader understands the importance of being loyal to the message.

FOR CONSIDERATION:

- What is to be gained by keeping staff disagreements behind closed doors?

- What are the advantages to staff staying on message?

- Can a staff constructively debate in private and still be of one mind once a decision is made?

- How does cohesion among an organization's leaders help the business?

The West Pointer Is the Company's Greatest Advocate

Over the years, I have become convinced that one of the most useful tools a leader can possess is the ability to stand in front of a large group of people and give a good speech. In recent years, the Academy has hosted leaders' conferences, where fund-raising, reunion planning, and alumni affairs are discussed at length. For me, the high points of these forums are unquestionably the meals—not because I've grown excessively fond of food over the years, but because these lunches and dinners invariably include West Point alumni speaking about something enthusiastically. It might be a military campaign fought with pride, or a charity event that is underway, or a change at the Academy that alumni either support or oppose. I'm usually enthralled: I love listening to an impassioned West Pointer speak in front of a group of people.

I'm not sure what it is about the West Point manner that lends itself to ardent public speaking. Perhaps it is the year spent reciting fourth-class knowledge to a highly critical audience that instills confidence and zeal in the cadet. Perhaps it has to do with having to explain math work on the blackboard before one's classmates and a scrutinizing professor. Maybe it comes from serving in the cadet leadership and having to convince one's fellow cadets to follow an endless list of Academy rules and instructions. After all, there's nothing tougher than managing one's peers. Whatever it is, it works, and I urge anyone who does not feel comfortable standing before an audience and stating a case to purchase a book or take a course on how to do it better.

But beyond the mechanics of good oratory, I suggest that what makes West Pointers convincing speakers is a deeply held passion for the message. These emotional advocators really *believe* what they're saying—and it shows. The persuasive speaker or manager has personalized the message before taking it to the audience, the organization, or the team.

Strong leaders often become fervent spokespeople for the company's vision. If they fill the role properly and express their loyalty from the heart, these people come across as devoted company members, rather than superficial self-servers. As they make a case for the organization's objectives, they are compelling and effective in the consistency of their message and the sure-minded arguments that support it. They filter through the organization, inspiring other people as well.

> *Strong leaders often become fervent spokespeople for the company's vision.*

The inspirational team leader frequently functions as an extension of the higher-up leadership, supporting the decisions that have been handed down from the top. If the higher-up leadership is equally motivating, then all levels of management have been asked for their input, and even if their ideas aren't bought into completely, they are part of the decision-making process and have the desire to support and defend the final resolutions.

I have been to every reunion my West Point class has held since graduation. Our class roster includes some Army leaders, accomplished engineers, successful businesspeople, aspiring politicians, and some very talented salespeople. During these reunions, when I ask classmates about whatever it is they're engaged in, they each talk about their occupations or projects with such passion that they sound evangelistic. They are clearly devoted to their calling and love to talk about it to others. I can not help but imagine how energized I would be if I belonged to any one of their teams.

The good leader takes the company's goals and visions personally. He is the quintessential "company man" without being superficially so.

FOR CONSIDERATION:

- Do you consider yourself an enthusiastic cheerleader for the organization?

- Are you comfortable describing your organization's vision in front of a group of people?

- Do you hold a passion for the things your organization wants you to carry out?

- How might you go about being a believer and campaigner for your boss?

- What are the benefits to being a strong advocate for your company and its goals?

The West Pointer Is the Soldier's Greatest Advocate

In one fashion or another, it has been proposed throughout this book that standing behind your "soldiers" is an effective approach for building trust and devotion. Let me emphasize the point: there is nothing more important to good leadership than being loyal to each member of your team and taking time for each member whenever appropriate.

History may be filled with examples of seemingly heartless, hard-nosed leadership. But, assuming the leadership was effective, I guarantee you that behind those supposedly autocratic masks were people who cared deeply for the members of their teams, especially the ones most in need of attention.

There are two reasons to serve as the soldier's greatest advocate. First, the time you take to publicly and privately support that person will come back to you tenfold. It is, indeed, a cold world out there and getting a lot colder, in my estimation. People at all levels of many organizations tend to appear self-serving and closed off. By differentiating yourself as that *one* manager willing to go out on a limb for someone or take time to help someone develop and advance, you foster the type of allegiance that lays the groundwork for transformational leadership. It is this type of leadership that brings about revolutionary change and improvement.

Second, serve as an advocate for the soldier because, at times, it is simply the right thing to do, and chances are you're the only one willing to do it. I can recall many times when an organization I was a part of—a military unit, a manufacturing group, or a college—had to make a thumbs-up or thumbs-down decision about someone on my team. Granted, I supported the thumbs-down decision when it was clearly warranted. But there were also those times when I saw something in the subject of a closed-door debate—a spark, a sign of potential, or a good heart—and I stuck my neck out in support of keeping him or her around. I fully understood that, if the decision went my way, I would be taking on something of a pet project in proving I was right.

The notion of advocacy calls to mind Henry Ossian Flipper, West Point Class of 1877, the first African American graduate of the Academy and one of only three black cadets to graduate prior to 1900. Henry Flipper was born into slavery in 1856 and, following the Civil War, was appointed for admission into the U.S. Military Academy. Considering how the war between North and South had divided the Academy, as well as the hazing and rigid academics any cadet of that era had to endure, one cannot help but wonder about the bitterness and hatred that

A good team leader serves as the soldier's strongest sponsor.

existed when New Cadet Flipper showed up at the Academy. One can imagine the challenges he had to face at the hands of cadets and officers who were eager to see him fail. I suspect that, in the name of ushering in a new time and seeing past the color of a person's skin, one or two people at West Point decided to endure the notoriety and hostility of serving as this new cadet's supporter. And I suspect that this sponsorship was the difference between an early departure and a historical achievement.

I spent some of my time as an Army officer looking for diamonds in the rough and serving as their promoter. As a cannon platoon leader, I insisted that a few of my soldiers consider advancing themselves as officer candidates in the Army. One of them went on to apply for admission to the Academy. One of the proudest moments of my life was attending his graduation seven years later.

A good team leader serves as the soldier's strongest sponsor. When a team member needs a supporter during a challenging, unsure time, the true leader is always there to speak up on his behalf.

FOR CONSIDERATION:

- Can you think of a time when you stuck your neck out for someone on your team? Are you glad you did?

- What is to be gained from serving as an advocate for members of your team?

- Aside from perhaps receiving loyalty in return, what are the ethical reasons for serving as an advocate?

- Do you recall any proud moments of advocacy or encouragement?

The West Pointer Takes On the Lost Cause

Taking on a lost cause and turning defeat into victory is something of a common thread throughout the history of West Point graduates. A few examples of West Pointers turning around major setbacks already have been mentioned: MacArthur returning to the Bataan region of the Philippines after it was overtaken by Japanese forces in World War II; George Goethals taking on and completing the Panama Canal construction project after decades of failed attempts; Gregory Crouch's ascent of Cerro Torre's West Face in Patagonia during the winter after enduring earlier mountain climbing defeats. West Pointers not only love challenges; they embrace the crusades others have given up.

Frequently, there is another lost cause that the good leader tackles: the hopeless team. When a leader takes on the *team* that's a lost cause, he defines himself as someone who believes that people should not be pigeonholed into good and bad categories and that individuals can be molded and channeled into positive components of a team. The manager who accepts the challenge of the failing team is saying, "Yes, I *can* make a difference and this team *can* be effective."

One of the textbooks I studied as a cadet was *Small Unit Leadership*, written by Dandridge M. Malone, a retired Army colonel who was well-known in military circles for his training classes on practical leadership applications. Malone dedicates part of his book to discussing the lost cause group—the team with poor ability, low motivation, and a weak sense of collaboration. He calls the category "low skill, low will, low teamwork."

Malone suggests that the first important step in assuming control of the lost cause group is to concentrate on the individual skills of team members. Without the work proficiencies necessary to get the job done, the team is destined to be the weak link in the organization. To ensure appropriate training takes place, you should set clear standards and explain them, one-on-one, to each member of your team. If the team is large enough, form sub-teams and assign sub-team leaders, giving each of them responsibility for training their people. Reward the sub-team leader who shows progress.

Once work skills have improved, the good manager works on motivation by giving team members ownership of as much of the mission as possible. People hold an inherent need to belong and contribute, and making them an integral part of any solution boosts self-esteem, team confidence, and drive.

As for teamwork, Malone says that if a team is motivated but still collaborates poorly, this probably has more to do with coordination than with personalities. The solution is having the team practice those tasks that require several people to do several different things at once. That is, the team needs to be drilled, even if the task involves something more cerebral than machinery or service.

Upon my arrival as a shift supervisor with International Paper Company, I was promptly assigned to supervise Crew Four, a group of proud misfits who had somehow come together on one crew that, by all accounts, no one else wanted to deal with. As the junior foreman, I had no say in the matter and took on a team that many considered a lost

The good manager works on motivation by giving team members ownership of as much of the mission as possible.

cause. Their skills were sharp enough. In fact, nearly everything I learned about papermaking they taught me. As far as motivation and teamwork, well, there was some work to be done in those areas. But over the course of three years, that team worked together through some challenging manufacturing orders, and we definitely made some paper, occasionally breaking seventy-year-old production records on that old relic of a machine. By respecting the team, letting them own the shift, and keeping tabs on how they threaded a sheet of paper through the machine and how they pooled their resources as a team, I kept things moving along a lot better than they had in the past.

The West Pointer often takes on the lost cause or the rebel team, the challenge no one wants to deal with. To the West Pointer, that project becomes a trial, a case for personal development representing the idea that situations and people *can* change for the better.

FOR CONSIDERATION:

- Have you ever been asked to take on a lost cause? What happened?

- What is to be gained from taking charge of a lost-cause group?

- How do you see yourself handling a lost cause?

The West Pointer Balances Loyalty Up with Loyalty Down

May the ghosts of the Long Gray Line forgive me. While the United States Military Academy is about everything Army, I'm about to reveal what an impact a *Navy* officer had on my management outlook!

While I was a cadet at West Point, our class was visited by U.S. Navy Admiral Grace Hopper, sometimes referred to as "The Mother of the Computer." Her story and her words remain inspiring to me to this day.

Grace Hopper was a Vassar professor during World War II when she volunteered to become part of the WAVES (Women Accepted for Voluntary Emergency Service). Commissioned as a Navy lieutenant (jg), she joined a research team that developed, programmed, and made practical the Mark I, Mark II, and Mark III electromechanical computing machines. Computer folklore has it that she traced a computer glitch in one of the Mark computers to a moth stuck in a relay—thus coining the phrase "computer bug." After her successful work on the Marks, she joined the team that created the first commercial computer, the UNIVAC.

Hopper was one of the world's first computer software engineers. She is credited with inventing the compiler, a program that translates human language into computer language. Her efforts were the beginnings of computer codes, formulas, and subroutines, and they led to the creation of COBOL (Common Business-Oriented Language), the first computer language based on words instead of numbers.

Unaware of who Hopper was or her amazing contributions to modern technology, my West Point classmates and I were fairly amused at the sight of this diminutive, white-haired woman in a Navy uniform. Being good-natured, she acknowledged our amusement, admitting that earlier in the day people had mistaken her for an elevator operator at the hotel where she was staying.

And then Hopper told her wonderful story and we were enthralled. She peppered her lecture with stories and philosophies about leadership—something you might not expect from a pioneer mathematician. Clearly, Hopper was as much of a military person as she was a genius technician. She talked about gathering together the right people for a project, acknowledging and rewarding good performance, and accepting and learning from failure.

But most important, she revealed what she called "the secret to good loyalty." Hopper suggested that the effective team leader balances loyalty to the boss or the company with loyalty to the members of the team. "Loyalty up needs to equal loyalty down," she said. Her reasoning: if a manager is perceived as being too dedicated to the boss, he takes on the reputation of a "party-line manager," meaning that people will be less inclined to trust him, approach him, or work hard for him. On the other hand, Hopper suggested that if a boss's dedication leans too heavily toward the members of team, the manager assumes the reputation of "panderer" or "softy," and therefore loses the respect and trust of the company's senior leadership. The goal for the manager, therefore, is

The goal for the manager is constantly to balance dedication to the team with dedication to the company.

constantly to balance dedication to the team with dedication to the company. It also means, when possible, bridging the gaps between what the company desires and what the team desires.

Hopper died in 1992, seven years after I heard her speak at West Point. She was buried in Arlington National Cemetery.

I don't think there's a work philosophy I've followed more faithfully than hers. Balancing loyalty up with loyalty down; letting your boss and your company know you're dedicated to the visions and goals of the organization, and letting your team know you're dedicated to their interests and concerns to the point where they'll return the loyalty and the effort.

FOR CONSIDERATION:

- In your day-to-day management routine, are you able to balance your loyalty to your boss and your company with your loyalty to your team?

- Why shouldn't a leader simply stay loyal to the boss? After all, it's the boss who signs the paychecks and writes the annual evaluations. What is to be gained by showing equal loyalty to subordinates?

- What might happen if a leader chooses to be too strong an advocate for the team, and seems to care more about the team than the wishes of the boss or the company?

- Balancing your loyalty is a constant juggling feat. What is the reward for staying in this constant state of shifting equilibrium?

Believe It or Not, the West Pointer Has a Sense of Humor

It sounds like a miserable predicament, always having to choose sides and balance loyalties. After reading this chapter on allegiance, you might wonder if being a good manager is something of a depressing undertaking, a situation where the best you can hope for is to keep everyone equally dissatisfied. You would think that these endless dilemmas would make for a relatively unhappy existence.

On the contrary, West Pointers are a generally upbeat bunch, accepting management quandaries in lighthearted ways. Uttering the phrase, "It's never over" whenever a predicament seems likely to persist (and most of them do), cadets are probably better at laughing off a situation than anyone. With a touch of humor, a wisecracking remark, and perhaps even a practical joke or two, cadets carry on through four long years with smiles.

West Pointer Scott Zigmond remembers handling a tough part of cadet life with a dose of humor. He recalls how little sleep he got while he was at the Academy and how draining that was physically and mentally, especially during his plebe year. Zigmond figured that an easy way to combat the lack of sleep and perk up a bit would be to laugh along with his comrades at cadets dozing off in class.

"It became something of a sport," says Zigmond. "We'd sit there and watch each other's eyelids going heavy, until someone went out completely, head dropping—sometimes snapping so hard it would hit the desk. The goal was to be the one laughing, and not the one laughed at!"

As it turned out, there was a lesson to be found in this humorous activity of sleep watching. "It was first semester plebe year," recollects Zigmond. "We were all required to present our math work on the board. I was giving some type of presentation to the class. I remember looking over and seeing one of my classmates sound asleep while I was up there presenting. With the professor and everyone else smiling approvingly, I took one of the blackboard erasers and threw it in his direction. It didn't hit him, but it struck close enough to startle him awake. Everyone laughed, and I continued on with my presentation."

After he was done reviewing his work on the board, Zigmond took his seat. "About thirty minutes later, someone else was presenting—and guess who fell asleep? You've got it. I did. And guess what the presenter threw at me? That's right—an eraser that bounced right off my head! It was absolutely one of the most humbling experiences I had ever had in a short eighteen years. This story doesn't exactly cast me in a great light, I suppose, but that's what laughing and learning is all about, right?"

Leaders shouldn't take themselves too seriously.

In fact, Zigmond says that his amusing experience in that classroom set a baseline for addressing people empathetically as a manager. He says that he learned to praise people in public and provide constructive criticism or tough coaching in private. "Leaders should never embarrass other people—throwing the eraser in front of others, so to speak. Leaders should maintain their humility. And they shouldn't take themselves too seriously."

These days, Zigmond is a business manager with Roche Diagnostics Corporation in Indianapolis. He says that he continues to share his funny cadet stories with his leadership team.

Addressing life with a dose of humor keeps the team appropriately relaxed and comfortable when handling tough situations. It provides wholesome stress relief during times that are otherwise taxing on body and spirit. And, most importantly, it acknowledges that no one is perfect. Accepting those imperfections through laughter is soothing and therapeutic.

Support for the team doesn't always have to be serious affair. Taking everything in the spirit of how silly life often gets keeps the team at ease and keeps the team leader mentally and physically healthy.

FOR CONSIDERATION:

- Has there been a recent predicament in your life that you approached with a touch of humor? What happened?

- How does a good sense of humor relate to good leadership?

- What sort of therapeutic quality does humor have?

CHAPTER TEN

CHANGE

BE TRANSFORMATIONAL

The West Pointer Serves as the Inspiration for Change

Human beings possess two prominent traits: a) they are creatures of habit, and b) they intensely fear the unknown. Therefore, it is no wonder that people dread the prospect of change and hate it while it is taking place. Such an aversion is unfortunate, however, because without change, there can be no progress. The organization that resists change is essentially setting the agenda for its own demise.

The transformational leader fights this resistance and becomes a catalyst for change within an organization. The West Pointer understands how this inspiration works and how it is utilized.

People outside of West Point tend to view the Academy as a rigid institution, devoid of evolution and new ideas. It is a stereotype that the Corps of Cadets plays along with. The satirical advertising slogan is: "West Point—200 years of tradition unhampered by progress!" The fact that the uniforms haven't changed much over that period of time plays into the delusion. However, anyone involved with the Academy knows that everything about West Point—its leadership development system, its academic requirements, its forms of punishment and rewards, its restrictions and privileges—is in a constant state of flux. To most "old grads," any change amounts to nothing more than the Corps going to hell. But once the curmudgeon instinct subsides, they realize that these changes are—for the most part—improvements, necessary for the evolution of the Academy and our nation's defense.

As it turns out, while new policies are constantly being introduced to cadets, it is the cadet leadership that has to instruct the Corps to accept these changes and follow them. It is a process that takes talent and technique. I would suggest that selling cadets on a new policy to the point where they eventually care intensely about its outcome is similar to selling a product to customers. Some of the best salespeople I know personally are Academy graduates, and they follow a few basic steps in getting people to embrace change.

The effective leader pushes the need for change in the role of an enthusiastic, convincing agent.

First, to get people on board, you must establish a need. If team members do not perceive or understand the need for a change or a mission, then there's a likelihood they will not accept it. As many a good salesperson will tell you, no need equals no sale.

Second, the employees (the customers) need to sense that they're getting a good deal. Generally, what's good for the team is good for its members, but people sometimes need to be sold on why this is so. You have to explain to them why they either will ultimately benefit from a change or a project, or what sort of adversity they'll endure by not caring.

Third, when selling team members on a change or a project, you have to push past their passivity. Remember, an object moving in a particular direction continues to do so unless it's met with resistance or force from another direction. Your conviction must possess enough force to overcome people's tendency to keep doing things the same old way.

Fourth, you need to address your customers' underlying expectation of reciprocation. That is, after convincing them that a real need exists and that it's worth it for them to respond with energy and motivation, you need to take the further step of ensuring your team members that their contribution will result in direct benefits in return.

Fifth, any good sales pitch includes a reference to scarcity. "Sale lasts only one more day!" "Only three items left!" Don't make up stories of scarcity when selling an objective to your team. But do suggest truthfully that the ability for them to contribute to a solution depends on the success of that solution. In other words, once a team fails and people are playing catch-up or clean-up, the members of the team are less likely to have a say in how things are accomplished. Contributing ideas and input on how a team gets the job done is restricted to those members of teams that succeed.

Finally, don't ever confuse the difference between your team's ability and its *willingness* to jump on board. Just because your team members have the experience and intelligence to offer their input and support, you can't just assume it will happen. Team buy-in is best demonstrated by early actions and results.

Selling change to an organization is like marketing a product to the public. The effective leader pushes the need for change in the role of an enthusiastic, convincing agent.

FOR CONSIDERATION:

- Why do people tend to fight change?

- What was a recent change in your organization that everyone resisted, but that ended up being a much-needed improvement?

- What might be gained from selling your team members on the need for change rather than imposing it on them?

- How might you go about selling your team on the need for change?

West Pointers Make People Want to Please Them

If selling people on the need for change is the tangible part of the transformational leadership process, then instilling in them a deep desire to change is the elusive part.

In the military, it's not uncommon for a veteran to look back at his combat experience and his commander and sincerely claim, "I would have died for that man." History books are packed with accounts of soldiers accomplishing amazing feats in the face of death because of their professed devotion to their commanding officer.

That's what transformational leadership is all about: inspiring people to do extraordinary things, sometimes for no other reason than to gain the approval of their leader. It doesn't require brainwashing or good looks or over-the-top charisma. More likely, it is a type of chemistry between a manager and his team that has been alluded to elsewhere in this text.

Some of the elements of devotion building have been previously mentioned: setting the example, respecting soldiers' abilities, being open with them, selling them on the need for change, showing them loyalty. Perhaps these elements are like the ingredients of a salad, and the charisma that creates deep, personal commitment is like the dressing that's poured over all of it. In other words, maybe it's possible to display and practice all the attributes of a great leader, but still be only a good leader—the salad that's okay but could use some vinaigrette.

Production manager Bob Doran says he believes the dressing on the salad to be a manager's ability to bridge the gap between the requirements of the organization and the desires of the workers. "Suppose the company has just handed you a rubbish sandwich," says Doran. "If you can present that sandwich in such a way that your team is inclined to eat it, then you can lead your department to greatness." He also believes that in order to build devotion, a manager must fight low morale before it takes root. "Whatever's getting people down has to be addressed and reversed before it takes over," he suggests.

As mentioned above, how a manager "sells" change to the team has a lot to do with how that team—and that manager—will thrive. Doran believes the devotion builder takes the sales pitch a few steps further. "This type of leader *celebrates* change," he says. "He treats change as if it were free money, as if it were the key to paradise." In celebrating change, Doran proposes, the leader creates a vision, and then he motivates people one-on-one until everybody's excited about the vision. This enthusiasm leads to training, implementation, and achievement. "I doubt if there's a greater sense of accomplishment in a company than the one felt when a leader's grand vision is promoted and carried out."

> *Transformational leadership is all about inspiring people to do extraordinary things.*

Supply and production manager Rich Vincz suggests that perhaps transformational leadership—getting to the point where your team wants to reassure you—is not as profound as it sounds. "Let them know what you're interested in and what will make you happy as a manager," he recommends. "Sometimes just being open about what you're priorities are and what changes you think are needed for the team is enough to get people to react."

When Douglas MacArthur first arrived at West Point as its superintendent in 1919, the post adjutant was Major William A. Ganoe, who, like many officers stationed at the Academy, thought MacArthur was much too young and unceremonious to fulfill the duties of superintendent. When MacArthur first met Ganoe, the major was completing his letter of resignation. MacArthur tore it up and convinced Ganoe he needed him around. The general told Ganoe what changes he thought were necessary and included Ganoe in making many early decisions. The major was not only converted, but eventually became devoted to MacArthur, venerating him and keeping historical notes on the general's tenure at West Point.

There are many examples of MacArthur's devotion-building, and they hint at an underlying premise: great leaders believe that people *can* be converted, and that meaningful change *can* be brought about.

You have become a transformational leader when people work hard for no other reason than a hope to impress and support you.

FOR CONSIDERATION:

- Have you ever had a manager who was so caring and charismatic that people went out of their way to accomplish things for this boss?

- What makes *you* want to please your boss?

- What tangible qualities might the devotion-building leader possess? What about the intangible qualities?

- What does promoting good morale have to do with devotion building?

- How does the process of selling change tie in with devotion building?

The West Pointer Knows How to Tell People to Go to Hell

Good leadership is the result of good investment—investment of time, energy, attention, nurture, and goodwill. Just as a mutual fund manager knows where to concentrate the investors' money on any particular day, the productive team leader knows where to channel a daily input of effort and enthusiasm.

Unfortunately, there are those times when managers discover that they're not getting a good return on their investments. Or, even worse, they realize that their investments are being wasted or abused. It can be a devastating feeling when you become aware that your goodwill is not being returned. Many managers, especially new ones, assume that input always equals output, and that dedication will always be mirrored. The discovery that one's boss, peers, or team members don't always reciprocate is discouraging.

But, if you are going to practice the type of leadership that involves passionate dedication to people and causes, it stands to reason that you will inevitably run across people who neither appreciate nor give back such passion. Moreover, probably those times will occur when people take advantage of your eagerness and your caring attitude.

Much of this book has centered on the West Pointer as the strong, yet compassionate, leader, a champion for the team member and the just cause. But make no mistake—West Pointers are considerate and at times benevolent, but they are no pushovers. I remember many times at the Academy when the cadet captain, realizing that his consideration for someone was being ignored by that person, said either through words or actions or both, "You've wasted my time, now go to hell!"

A few years ago, when I became a college adjunct instructor teaching economics, I was determined to show interest and compassion to each of my students. Within a few weeks, some students stopped showing up for class, and others failed to turn in assignments. They all had excuses that I initially bought, but eventually I realized that I was being had. And so, I began counting attendance toward their grades and I stopped offering make-up quizzes and assignments.

The smart leader knows how to voice displeasure, break off such a contact, and move on without entirely burning the bridge.

Attendance and assignment turn-ins went up, the number of excuses went down. I never said "go to hell," but I believe the students giving less than 100 percent got the message anyway.

Don't become disillusioned when people take advantage of your enthusiasm. The law of averages suggests that any team or organization is bound to have one or two people who find creative ways to test the boss. If it's a peer who's performing poorly, ignoring the person and concentrating your effort elsewhere is easy. If it's a team member, your actions probably should be accompanied by voicing your displeasure.

Don't rule out the possibility of bringing back your caring attitude if the person you've channeled your efforts away from comes around. Relationships are ever changing and so are people.

It's worth mentioning that political decency suggests that you don't *actually* tell someone to "go to hell." You'll end up burning a bridge you might need later on. Let your actions—particularly the redirecting of your time and energy—send the message. Also, think twice before acting if the person wasting your time is your superior. Telling the boss to go to hell, even indirectly through your actions, is probably not a smart thing unless you've put in your notice. Better to go and clarify with your supervisor what the priorities are and why your efforts are being used in a way that bothers you. The conversation may make you realize that your time is not being wasted as you think it is, or, if it's being wasted *exactly* as you think it is, the talk might prompt your director to reconsider how your resources could be better used.

People know when their time is being wasted or their good faith is being misused. The smart leader knows how to voice displeasure, break off such a contact, and move on without entirely burning the bridge.

FOR CONSIDERATION:

- Have you ever felt that your time and concern was being wasted? What did you do?

- Why is it important for a leader to have limits on how people take advantage of his time?

- How can you tell someone to "go to hell" without actually saying it? How can you send the message with your actions?

- Why is it important to keep open the possibility of someone returning to your good graces?

The West Pointer Avoids Worthless Meetings

Statistics suggest that half of every workday is spent in meetings and that half of all meeting time is useless. Surely there must be a better way to run a team and a more efficient way to manage one's time. The successful leader recognizes meetings for the hollow management vehicles they are and instead embraces a philosophy of one-on-one communication, delegating, and hands-on leadership.

The United States Army is unfortunately a meeting-riddled culture, and West Point is no different. Some of the longest, most mind-numbing meetings I ever attended—meetings that took up precious cadet time—were those called by our tactical officers (or TACs), the full-time Army officers on hand to develop our military skills. Those get-togethers were often excruciating, covering mundane topics such as Academy policies and inspection procedures. As I've mentioned above, many of the best lessons I learned at the Academy were not part of the curriculum. Thanks to dreary gatherings with my TACs, the general uselessness of meetings was one of them.

> *The successful leader recognizes meetings for the hollow management vehicles they are and instead embraces a philosophy of one-on-one communication, delegating, and hands-on leadership.*

Interestingly enough, the culture of meetings very often ended with the TACs, and meetingless management often began with the Corps of Cadets. Looking back, it seems to me that the Corps was a place where communication was streamlined and personal and where strong leadership and decision-making took the place of conference room fluff. At the Academy, cadet captains made straightforward choices, gave commands, and sent their colleagues on their way to get things done. And if they needed feedback, they personally went and asked people, honing their listening skills in the process of gathering advice. And, of those meetings I do recall among cadets, I remember their fast, no-nonsense nature. There wasn't anything revolutionary about this stripped-down approach: we simply didn't have time for long, laborious conferences.

In some ways, the Corps was like an ant colony, where communication traveled in a line, undiluted, from being to being. The long-winded meeting was scarce—the mindless lunch meeting was nonexistent.

This colony of workers was devoid of office cubicles and conference rooms. Rarely did one spot more than two cadets together in one place. There was no water-cooler talk. The pressure placed on cadets' schedules dictated that there was no time for people to travel and gather. Congregating was inefficient. One-on-one communication took over.

The result was a work environment where everyone was instantly accessible. Cadet captains did not have to call business meetings just to track down their key players. Colleagues didn't have to call meetings to gather important information for a project. The Corps simply went about its business and guidance was passed out directly to each cadet, tailored to that particular person's requirements and demands.

In the Corps, the delegating of tasks replaced the need for the daily morning meeting. And as cadet captains made their way through this ant colony, encountering their team members along the way, everyone got a chance to hear pertinent data and offer feedback. Since, at that moment, they had their commander's exclusive attention, the communication was stronger and more meaningful. The interesting irony about this type of one-on-one management was that cadet captains were *saving* time by communicating with their team members one at a time. Mathematically and functionally, it made sense. It took less time to talk to ten individuals for five minutes at a time than to congregate all ten of them for an hour—and individual communication was more effectual, more real.

Finally, since cadets rarely found the time to form groups larger than two, there was little danger of "groupthink," the conference-room condition where awful ideas take over a group and everyone buys into them in the name of conformity. To be sure, bad ideas sometimes *did* take on lives of their own at the Academy—the ideas generated in those TAC meetings, previously mentioned.

As a West Pointer, I carried my disdain for meetings into my military career and into business, observing and emulating those rare and highly effective leaders who managed just fine without conference room get-togethers.

The four best bosses—military and civilian—I have ever worked for made decisions and showed the way with few, if any, meetings. I have tried to follow this wonderful way of leading people.

The good leader likes to explain the mission and set good people free to do great things. Pulling people into meetings usually means poor use of time and defective "groupthink" decision-making.

FOR CONSIDERATION:

- Do you find yourself overwhelmed by meetings, including the ones that you convene?

- Have you ever watched a really bad idea take over the conference room? What happened?

- What is to be gained from getting together with your team members individually rather than taking up their time in a conference room?

- Why is the strong leader less inclined to feel the need to convene a meeting?

- What leadership tools can appropriately replace endless meetings?

The West Pointer Doesn't Want to Be Larger Than Life, But Full of Life

When discussing West Point icons like Eisenhower, MacArthur, and Patton, it is easy to fall into the presumption that all great leaders have a special star quality. Looking back, certain images come to mind, such as the Eisenhower golf swing, the MacArthur sunglasses and pipe, and the Patton riding crop. One thinks of Norman Schwarzkopf's *tour de force* press briefing at the tail end of Operation Desert Storm. These images are somewhat endearing in different ways and certainly enduring.

The problem with these pictures, however, is that they fall into the same category as Pete Townshend's guitar smashing or Marilyn Monroe's skirt blowing up. They hint at an idolized status that most of us wouldn't relish and that the vast majority of us will never attain.

Unfortunately, these images also imply that an incredibly large ego is necessary to be a talented leader. The unspoken suggestion is that people who aspire toward greatness must first be full of themselves before starting their grand campaign. It's understandable that some people, holding humility as an important trait, shun such loftiness.

The reality of good leadership is that having a larger-than-life status or opinion of yourself is not necessary and, in plenty of cases, potentially counterproductive. The manager who enters a situation with a surefooted, yet unassuming, approach is just as likely to gain team support and influence people in an industrious way. It was mentioned above that the best warriors are often the most unlikely warriors. The same can be said for leaders. Many times I have met the leader of a department or company and thought to myself, "Now, what on earth is *this* person doing managing an organization?" only to be stunned later on by the person's influence over people, events, and business. Don't give in to appearance and prejudge someone's ability to lead based on how they look or sound.

As for West Pointers, the Academy graduate often is a well-presented, vibrant personality. And, yes, history books contain lots of stories about colorful West Point alumni. But I would argue that for each over-the-top icon, there are thousands of West Point leaders who go about the business of getting things done in very low-key fashion. Confident? Yes. Energetic and animated? You bet. But not egotistical or pompous. These down-to-earth graduates make up the bulk of the Long Gray Line.

The friendly, unpretentious, wholehearted approach is personified by my West Point classmate, Dave Clonts. Clonts is a major in the U.S. Army who went back to teach at West Point some years after graduation. A tall, imposing infantry officer, he easily could have chosen an overbearing, showy style of managing. Indeed, some of the assignments he has been given in the Army would have justified this approach. By all accounts, Clonts maintains effective control over his staff and his soldiers but he appears to be anything but self-important. Clonts has a loud, infectious laugh that is instantly disarming. While he is demanding of those around him, his caring

The reality of good leadership is that having a larger-than-life status or opinion of yourself is not necessary and, in plenty of cases, counterproductive.

tone, occasionally joking manner, and passion for living make people want to follow him. I suspect that if I were to work for Dave, he could talk me into walking off a cliff.

Enthusiasm is probably the common thread running through all types of good leadership styles. My first writing experience as a student was being taught how to write news copy by a great communications teacher, John Jeppi. Jeppi was full of little catchy sayings that had a way of sticking in my mind. My favorite was his assertion that "If you act enthusiastic, you'll *be* enthusiastic!" His notion was that if you go into a situation that you'd rather not be a part of, but feign passion for the sake of the team, this excitement will be contagious and will wind up coming back to you as *real* enthusiasm. Over twenty years later, I use this philosophy all the time and it is a wonderful management tool.

Although your leadership approach needs to be tailored to your situation and, to a large extent, your personality, the appropriate method for you in all likelihood will involve a suitable mix of confidence, zest, cheerleading, and humility. You might be the spellbinding star who leads your team with fanfare. Or you might be the quiet, sure leader who takes your team to new heights.

Perhaps some people in charge prefer the icon-like status of MacArthur or Patton. But good leaders generally don't need or desire prima donna status. They would much rather fill a business office with life, energy, and enthusiasm than with ego.

FOR CONSIDERATION:
- Is it possible to be a great leader without being "larger than life"?

- How might you go about displaying a high-energy, vivacious persona?

- How might you go about injecting energy into your team's work environment?

- Is it possible that feigning enthusiasm might *create* genuine enthusiasm?

The West Pointer Knows
the "Bucket of Water" Analogy

When I was a cadet at West Point, one of my professors told the class that a well-run organization is like a bucket of water.

When your hand is in the bucket, you are very much a part of what's going on in there. Your hand swishes around, splashing the water and causing all kinds of activity. But when you're not around and people look at the bucket, there's really no indication that you had put your hand in it. The bucket of water stands on its own, looking much as it did before you were a part of it.

So it is with the manager of a strong organization. When you are at a robust company, you are an integral part of it, contributing ideas and making good things happen. But when you're away—on vacation or off to another assignment—the group continues on as if you had never shown up from the start.

Carry the analogy further. Suppose there's a leak in bucket and your finger plugs the hole. If you were to leave, the water would be lost. Suppose your hand is less than clean. If you were to leave, the water would be dirty.

My West Point professor was making a good point. The conscientious leader wants the organization to function not only when she's around, but also when she's *not* around. A manager that is so intertwined in the daily mundane activities of the company can neither set people free to get things done nor concentrate on the bigger issues of the day. Micro-managing might give a boss a false sense of control, but in effect it's the tasks that end up running the manager, not the other way around.

Keeping in mind that people trust steady organizations, the conscientious leader does not want to radically alter the company that is competently carrying out its mission. At some point, everyone has worked for the supervisor who seeks change for the sake of change or, worse still, change for the sake of gaining attention. Self-promotion is one thing, but creating sweeping projects for personal publicity becomes a drain on resources and is potentially bad for the business. If the group is headed in the right direction, it needs to stay pointed that way.

If a leader has been asked to repair a damaged organization—the leaking bucket—the restoration must be such that the leader can leave when it's done. Rather than plugging the bucket hole with a finger, the leader should use a sealant that will do the trick regardless of who's around. That's not to say that a leader shouldn't remain on hand through-

If your people do a good job when you're not around, it says as much about you as it does about them.

out the resolution and even after its completion, but if the fix goes away when the leader does, then the remedy was never really corrective to begin with.

Working in the company, the leader should "keep her hands clean," maintaining a level of integrity and good faith that keeps the organization from suffering the tarnish of deceitfulness or scandal. If someone can look at the water bucket and tell that your filthy fingers were in there, then you have failed miserably at being a principled supervisor.

The bucket analogy made for an important lesson at West Point, where officers and cadets were responsible for getting the job done within the confines of a highly regarded institution while maintaining its reputation and keeping it on track. Much as with the bucket of water, the Academy would still function at the same level before and after good leaders came through it and made their contributions. The lesson alludes to another good point: if your people do a good job when you're not around, it says as much about you as it does about them.

Fraud prevention manager John Barry appreciates the analogy. "The point is that when you manage people, everyone should be of the same mindset, concentrating on the same goals. If people share the same professionalism and dedication, then the manager can leave without things falling apart. The bucket of water hasn't changed."

A good leader can leave the office knowing that the team is strong enough to run without him.

FOR CONSIDERATION:
- Why should you be concerned with how an organization functions when you're away?

- Why should you care about what happens to an organization after you have left it for another assignment or opportunity?

- Have you ever worked for a micromanager? What was your assessment of that person's routine and outlook?

- What other situations can you add to the "bucket of water" analogy?

The West Pointer Longs to Make a Difference

I entered the United States Military Academy as the oldest member of my class. At twenty-one years and three hundred sixty days old, I was five days under West Point's inflexible upper-age limit of twenty-two (the Academy's upper-age limit has since been increased to twenty-three).

Having been accepted into the Academy out of the Army's enlisted ranks, I was neither a high-school valedictorian nor a high-school team captain—distinctions belonging to many cadets. I was short and dumpy, with a soldier's mouth and insolent humor, and the last two would get me into plenty of trouble over the next four years.

It is no wonder that, during my yearling year, the classmates in my cadet company secretly signed a petition nominating me for class president. If nothing else, I'd be good for a laugh!

There must have been some disbelief among them when I accepted their nomination and seriously began to run for the office. After an elimination vote and a run-off election, I was elected class president. It was a position I discharged for three years at the Academy, helping to plan events such as 100th Night Weekend, when my classmates celebrated the one hundred day count until graduation, and Graduation Week itself, the week that we tossed our hats into the air as a proud members of West Point's Long Gray Line.

I carried the job of class president past graduation, planning three reunions and helping to organize a class gift endowment to the Academy. On an item-by-item basis, I really take very little credit for any of the class's accomplishments before or since graduation: there was always a wonderful person willing to chair a committee or take on a class cause. But if people said yes because I asked, and if I helped serve as the glue that held much of it together, then it is easily the thing I am more proud of than all other life successes put together.

My reasoning for accepting the nomination when it had started out as a goof was simple: I wanted to make a difference. If I had learned nothing else during that early time at the Academy, I had quickly discovered that leadership was all about having a deep desire to make a positive impact on a team or an organization. And upon learning it, I had internalized it—I longed to make a difference.

Great managers gravitate toward the seemingly insurmountable role of leader because they not only want to make a difference, but they long to do so.

Such a philosophy, at first glance, seems silly in today's business world. People make careers out of maintaining the status quo. Besides, making a difference means extra work and extra responsibility—notions that run contrary to those who instinctively hand off assignments to coworkers.

People wanting to make a difference are an endangered species in today's business world. The person who willingly takes on a crusade is sometimes seen as a punching bag—as something of a chump. What a shame. Wonderful challenges and successes await the businessperson willing to step up to the plate. Certainly you have your saturation point, but to the extent that all organizations are dynamic and that change brings new challenges and new crusades, you should seek to be first in line to take them on.

And so, this book ends the same way it began—with the argument that you should always *seek responsibility*. Ask for more responsibility in the form of additional projects and accountability. Raise your hand when volunteers are sought.

Others around you might inwardly chuckle, but you'll have the last laugh when your success with a big undertaking makes you shine. Furthermore, if this new project is important enough, you will have a hand in charting a new course for the organization—a course that suits your outlook and liking.

My father, an old Marine Corps artilleryman, always used to say, "Remember, son, as long as you're in the military, never volunteer for anything!" But he never really meant it. I would learn later in life that my father had volunteered for one or two very special assignments in his day. As I was growing up, I remember my father as *the* quintessential volunteer, running church events and organizing talent shows year after year to raise money for our school.

Great managers gravitate toward the seemingly insurmountable role of leader because they not only want to make a difference, but they long to do so.

FOR CONSIDERATION:

- Do you truly long to make a difference?

- What are the reasons that might make you want to bring about a positive change or begin a long crusade?

- What is to be gained by taking on a crusade?

- What famous people have brought about revolutionary change simply by wanting to bring about positive change?

CONCLUSION

The "Alma Mater," West Point's beloved school song composed in 1908, includes these words:

And when our work is done,
Our course on earth is run,
May it be said, "Well done;
Be thou at peace."

It is a pleasant spring day at the Academy. The post is unusually quiet because nearly everyone stationed there or visiting has gathered in one place—Michie Stadium. The giant cement structure offsets the adjacent, woodsy solitude of Lusk Reservoir ("Which holds seventy-eight million gallons, sir, when the water is flowing over the spillway"). The arena is crackling with excited energy, packed with staff, dignitaries, families, spectators, and the United States Corps of Cadets. The Corps takes up only three-quarters of the bleacher seats it normally does. The other quarter—about a thousand of them—is seated on the football field in white chairs facing a makeshift stage. They are the first-class cadets. The end of one journey and the beginning of another are only moments away.

A curious mix of young children and enlisted soldiers are crowded at one end of the field, waiting anxiously behind a row of military police. The children and the soldiers are each on different missions.

The first-class cadets, now officially graduates of the United States Military Academy, stand up at attention. Their left hands hold diplomas and their right hands are free for cap tossing and saluting.

The superintendent of the Academy, a three-star general, instructs the first captain, the senior ranking member of the Corps, to officially dismiss this group of new Army second lieutenants. The first captain salutes and executes an about-face. He now faces his classmates. A hush goes over the stadium. He offers a proud bellow. "Class—*dismissed!*"

A thousand white caps fly into the air as the stadium erupts with cheers. The MPs allow the children and the soldiers onto the field. The children run furiously, gathering caps as souvenirs. A determined kid can leave the stadium with many caps.

The soldiers move methodically to as many graduates as possible, snapping salutes along the way. "Congratulations, sir." "Congratulations, ma'am." Each graduate returns the salute and removes a silver dollar from inside his or her left glove. It is a West Point tradition for each new graduate to offer a dollar to the first person who renders a salute. A determined soldier can leave the stadium with many silver dollars.

I'm in that stadium, nearly in tears, during this thrilling day. It is not my Graduation Day; my graduation happened seven years ago, in the same place, during a rainy outdoor mess that was still just as exhilarating. On this much sunnier day, I'm watching the graduation of Steven Olson, a former enlisted soldier from my cannon platoon whom I had persuaded to apply to the Academy. Further demonstrating that the Army is a small world (heck, the *world* is a small world), our former artillery brigade commander, Colonel Freddy McFarren, is on the stage. He's now *General* McFarren, a one-star general and the commandant of cadets.

I make my way onto the field after some of the mayhem has died down. Olson spots me and approaches. He looks very sharp and, although I'm wearing civilian clothes, I feel compelled to render a salute. "Congratulations, Lieutenant Olson."

He returns the salute and produces a silver dollar from his left glove. "I was hoping you'd be the one I'd hand this coin to," he says.

I initially hesitate. "That's for a soldier."

Lieutenant Olson keeps his hand stretched out. "I insist, sir." I take the coin, say hello to Olson's family, and leave the Academy that day with an overwhelming sense of fulfillment that I was able to pass along the mentoring that someone had given me as a soldier a dozen years before.

Ultimately, the sign of any well-managed organization is the consistency and continuity of its leadership. When you mold the potential of the people on your team, you not only receive the skills and goodwill of those you have developed, but you place the team on a straight path, allowing its members to further the organization for years to come as future managers and innovators.

A well-led institution also has predictable leadership. If a company is being skillfully supervised, you can conjecture what its managers are doing and what they are likely to do next. Such predictability, like tradition, is reassuring and affirming.

For example, one can surmise that, on any given evening at the Academy, a cadet captain wraps up the day with a million things on his mind. He goes for a run, by himself, hoping to push himself a little harder and finish the run a little faster. And he hopes the night air might streamline his cluttered thoughts and clear his focus. The first part of his route takes him past the statue of General MacArthur, reminding him that sometimes a leader must accept and rise to his near-crushing responsibilities. It has been said that we don't find crusades—they find us. This young cadet captain, responsible for about a hundred other cadets of different ranks and classes, is beginning to understand this notion.

He runs past the homes of the superintendent and the commandant, prompting him to ponder every utterance he has made that day. Were the statements truthful? Would scrutiny from these two generals uncover any half-truths or hidden agendas? He continues on, satisfied that he has lived another day with his integrity intact.

His run takes him along Washington Road and past the West Point Cemetery, where departed graduates are buried and where the span of the Long Gray Line is most physically pronounced in one place. He glances over at the sea of weathered headstones, marking the generations of graduates who, in their day, were dedicated to their country and were committed— even to the point of dying—to the concept that they were part of something bigger and more important than each of them.

Although the day has been long, he pushes himself to Washington Gate. There's no one around to notice. But his task is to reach the gate before turning back. At that very moment, it is the only task he is living and working to complete. He must reach the gate. And he does, touching it for self-assurance before turning around and completing the second half of his run.

As he returns to his barracks, he slows to a walk, checking the chronometer on his watch. Two seconds better than last time—yes!

He heads up toward his room, stopping first at another room housing three fourth-class cadets—plebes—two of them struggling academically. "How is calculus treating you?"

"Fine, sir."

"I trust the two of you visited your 'P' this week to plot out the second half of this semester."

"Yes, sir."

Looking at the third plebe: "And I trust you're helping out these two whenever you can."

"Yes, sir."

"Good. If things head downward grade-wise, I want to know about it. Got it?"

"Yes, sir."

"Good night."

"Good night, sir."

The fourth-class cadets intuitively notice their commander's appearance as he departs the room, leaving a puddle of sweat behind. Clearly, he cares about his physical condition and wants others to care about theirs. He has defined himself and, without consciously intending to, he has influenced others with his actions.

The cadet captain notices that his company's general areas look very clean—not always a given, even at the Academy. "Maybe I'll invite the TAC for a walk-through," he thinks to himself, understanding the value of good timing.

He reaches his room, drenched in sweat and covered with the pasty grime that sometimes comes along with New York State humidity. The run is over. "No, it's not," he thinks to himself. "It's never *really* over." But that's okay, because although the big picture, what lies on the horizon, is always changing and transforming, he has been instrumental—through small victories and successes along the way—in channeling this transformation.

After showering, he kicks back at his desk with his *Bugle Notes*, a small book filled with useful Army information and West Point lore. His intention is to refresh himself on a subject or two well enough to quiz several fourth-class cadets tomorrow. He studies three pages of Army medals and names them all aloud without second-guessing. While he would rather quiz the plebes on West Point lore, the TAC wants the emphasis to be on Army knowledge, and he feels as loyal to the TAC as he does to the plebes he wants to teach.

Before lying down, he stands in front of a full-length mirror, alone, self-critical of the body and spirit. His course on earth has just begun. But for this one day, he acknowledges to himself, he has mastered his universe.

SOURCE NOTES

Introduction

George S. Patton's reference to West Point as a holy place is mentioned in a wonderful, historical write-up about the Academy by Bruce Ollstein. The essay appears at the beginning of the *West Point Catalogue 1998–1999* (West Point, NY: U.S. Military Academy, 1997).

The Princeton Review's "Toughest to Get Into" college rankings are listed in its methodical college guide, *The Best 351 Colleges, 2004 Edition* (New York: Random House/Princeton Review imprint, 2003), by Robert Franek, Tom Meltzer, et al.

The stories of many prominent West Pointers are well known. However, I found out about Francis Greene, Horace Porter, and several other less recognized names during my visit to the temporary exhibition "West Point in the Making of America 1802–1918" at the Smithsonian Institution's National Museum of American History in Washington, D.C. The Institution's Barton C. Hacker and Margaret Vining published a companion book to the exhibition entitled *West Point in the Making of America* (Irvington, NY: Hydra, 2002).

Menoher's observation about MacArthur during World War I is mentioned in William Manchester's biographical text *American Caesar: Douglas MacArthur 1880–1964* (New York: Bantam Dell, 1983).

Chapter 1

The history of E. I. du Pont de Nemours and Company is presented in Adrian Kinnane's *Dupont: From the Banks of the*

Brandywine to Miracles of Science (Baltimore, MD: Johns Hopkins University Press, 2002). Information also is available at the Dupont website: heritage.dupont.com.

The West Pointer's custom of not making excuses for any reason is discussed in *Bugle Notes,* a small book containing much of the information new cadets need to have on hand. The version I used for writing this book was the one from my cadet days, *Bugle Notes (76th Volume)* (West Point, NY: U.S. Military Academy, 1984), written and compiled by the Academy's Staff of 1984.

Schwarzkopf's autobiography is *It Doesn't Take a Hero: The Autobiography* (New York: Bantam, 1992), by H. Norman Schwarzkopf with Peter Petre.

Chapter 2

Sylvanus Thayer is mentioned in *West Point in the Making of America*. The Honor Code is discussed along with the Three Rules of Thumb in *Bugle Notes*.

Douglas MacArthur's innovations while he was superintendent at West Point are referred to in *American Caesar*.

Information on the M247 Division Air Defense (DIVAD) gun debacle is available from the Federation of American Scientists at its website: www.fas.org.

The Nixon presidency's ethical undoing is described in Michael A. Genovese's book *The Watergate Crisis* (Westport, Connecticut: Greenwood Press, 1999).

Chapter 3

Abraham Maslow's superb biography is *The Right to be Human: A Biography of Abraham Maslow* (Los Angeles: Tarcher/New York: St. Martin's Press, 1988), by Edward Hoffman.

More about Robert Anderson can be found in Shelby Foote's exhaustive Civil War account, *The Civil War: A Narrative, Vol. I Fort Sumter to Perryville* (New York: Random House Vintage Books, 1986). Anderson also is mentioned in *West Point in the Making of America*.

The Airborne Creed (or Parachutist's Creed) is discussed in Peter Karsten's military textbook *The Training and Socializing of Military Personnel* (New York: Garland Publishing, 1998). Information also is available at Fort Bragg's website: www.bragg.army.mil.

Chapter 4

George W. Goethals and the rousing account of his overseeing the Panama Canal project are in a book written by his great-grandson, George R. Goethals, and columnist William Friar. The book is *Portrait of the Panama Canal: From Construction to the Twenty-First Century* (Portland, OR: Graphic Arts Center Publishing, 2003).

Chapter 5

Michael Ramundo's no-nonsense management book is *The Complete Idiot's Guide to Motivating People* (Indianapolis, IN: Alpha, 2000).

Gus Pagonis's inspiring leadership book is *Moving Mountains: Lessons in Leadership and Logistics from the Gulf War* (Boston: Harvard Business School Press, 1992), by William G. Pagonis with Jeffrey L. Cruikshank.

Carl R. Rogers discusses his counseling technique—an active listening process involving the "reflection of attitudes"—in his psychology text *Client-Centered Therapy* (New York: Houghton Mifflin, 1951).

Douglas MacArthur's observation about training is noted in *American Caesar*.

The principle of leadership on training is covered in *Bugle Notes*.

Dwight D. Eisenhower's farming analogy is mentioned in the book *Words From Our Presidents: Quips and Quotes from George Washington to George W. Bush* (New York: Gramercy, 2001), edited by Trevor Hunt.

Chapter 6

The Patton anecdote is cited by Richard Marcinko—the controversial United States counterterrorist commander—in his compelling leadership book, *The Rogue Warrior's Strategy for Success* (New York: Pocket Books, 1998). For other Patton leadership stories, I like Alan Axelrod's easy, inspiring read *Patton on Leadership: Strategic Lessons for Corporate Warfare* (Upper Saddle River, NJ: Prentice Hall Press, 1999).

John Sedgwick shows up frequently in Shelby Foote's *The Civil War: A Narrative, Vol. III Red River to Appomattox* (New York: Random House Vintage Books, 1986).

Chapter 7

Information on the competitive sport of orienteering is covered in detail by Steven Boga in his handbook *Orienteering: The Sport of Navigating with Map & Compass* (Mechanicsburg, PA: Stackpole Books, 1997).

Gregory Crouch's exciting book about mountain climbing and perseverance is *Enduring Patagonia* (New York: Random House, 2001).

Jason Jennings and Laurence Haughton's business book is *It's Not the Big That Eat the Small...It's the Fast That Eat the Slow: How to Use Speed as a Competitive Tool in Business* (New York: HarperBusiness, 2002).

Information about Tim Leatherman's success story is available at the Leatherman Tool Group's website: leatherman.com.

The Wal-Mart example of using *economies of scale* is discussed in the textbook *Economics (Second Edition)* (New York: Worth, 2000), by Timothy Tregarthen and Libby Rittenberg. Information and web links related to Wal-Mart's success story are available at Wal-Mart's website: walmartstores.com.

John I. Alger's military textbook is *Definitions and Doctrine of the Military Art: Past and Present* (Wayne, NJ: Avery, 1985).

Chapter 8

The West Point leadership principles on seeking self-improvement and being proficient are described in *Bugle Notes*.

Chapter 9

Henry Ossian Flipper's collected writings appear in *Black Frontiersman: The Memoirs of Henry O. Flipper, First Black Graduate of West Point* (Fort Worth, TX: Texas Christian University Press, 1997), by Henry Ossian Flipper and Theodore D. Harris.

Dandridge M. Malone's military textbook is *Small Unit Leadership: A Commonsense Approach* (Novato, CA: Presidio, 1983).

Information on Grace Hopper is available at the Grace Hopper Celebration of Women in Computing website: www.gracehopper.org. The annual event is presented by the Anita Borg Institute for Women and Technology and the Association for Computing Machinery.

Chapter 10

The story about MacArthur gaining the loyalty of William Ganoe, who then kept historical records on the general, appears in *American Caesar.*

The concept of transformational leadership is described by Gary A. Yukl in his textbook, *Leadership in Organizations, Fifth Edition* (Englewood Cliffs, NJ: Prentice Hall, 2001). It remains my favorite book on leadership.

Conclusion

The excerpt from the "Alma Mater," West Point's school song, is taken from *Bugle Notes.*

In writing this book, I tried to address common threads at the Academy over recent decades. I learned about West Point during the Korean War era from several discussions with William O'Brien of Staten Island, New York, whose assignments around that time included guarding the gates at the Academy.

I learned about West Point during the Vietnam era primarily from the book *The Long Gray Line: The American Journey of West Point's Class of 1966* (Boston: Houghton Mifflin, 1989), by Rick Atkinson. It is the most moving historical account of any group of people I have ever read.

I was reminded about West Point during the Reagan era by Colonel Larry R. Donnithorne's book, *The West Point Way of Leadership* (New York: Currency Doubleday, 1993). I am personally grateful to Colonel Donnithorne, who offered me guidance when I began this project.

For information on West Point during the Clinton era and today, I referred to *Absolutely American: Four Years at West Point* (Boston: Houghton Mifflin, 2003), a firsthand, four-year narrative observation by David Lipsky. It was a great read—and things haven't changed *that* much.

ABOUT THE AUTHOR

Scott Snair is a business manager, writer, college instructor/administrator, and consultant/lecturer. He is president of the West Point Class of 1988 and served as a United States cannon platoon leader in Saudi Arabia and Iraq during the liberation of Kuwait in the early 1990s.

Scott has worked in sales, manufacturing, and logistics management with companies such as Bell Atlantic and International Paper. He has also written *Stop the Meeting I Want to Get Off!*, a text on the general uselessness of most business meetings.

He lives with his wife and children in Old Bridge, New Jersey.

INDEX

H

I

J

K

L